CANADIAN CITIZENSHIP TEST

Angelo Tropea

ISBN-13: 978-1456532666

EAN-10: 1456532669

Published by Angelo Tropea

For all immigrants...all over the world.

Le serment de citoyenneté	The Oath Of Citizenship
je jure (ou j'affirme solennellement) Que je serai fidèle Et porterai sincère allégeance à Sa Majesté la Reine Elizabeth Deux Reine du Canada À ses héritiers et successeurs Que j'observerai fidèlement les lois du Canada Et que je remplirai loyalement mes obligations de citoyen canadien.	I swear (or affirm) That I will be faithful And bear true allegiance To Her Majesty Queen Elizabeth the Second Queen of Canada Her Heirs and Successors And that I will faithfully observe The laws of Canada And fulfill my duties as a Canadian citizen

CONTENTS

SAMPLE TESTS

STEPPING STONES

When I was seven, I went with my uncle Domenico on a trip to visit relatives who lived in the nearby countryside. On the way there a stream crossed our path. The stream was just deep enough and wide enough to make me fearful that I would never reach the other side. I complained to my uncle that I was not strong enough or tall enough to wade across it, and that I would surely be swept away by the current.

My uncle smiled and placed his hand on my shoulder. He pointed to a series of boulders whose tops jutted out above the water line. He told me that they were not boulders, but stepping stones, placed there by people who had crossed this stream before. He said, "You can't jump the stream with just one leap, but you *can* step from one stone to another – until you reach the other side."

Although my legs trembled, I did as my uncle suggested. I stepped from one stepping stone to another until I landed on the opposite shore. That day I learned that even a hard and fearful task can be accomplished if done in small steps.

This book provides a series of "flash questions" to help you learn in small steps the subject matter of the citizenship test. They are presented by someone who has "crossed this stream before." Please use these "stepping stones" to help you reach your goal of becoming a proud and informed citizen of Canada.

———————

THE CANADIAN CITIZENSHIP TEST

Persons who wish to become Canadian citizens are required to take the citizenship test if they are between the ages of 18 and 54.

In addition to successfully communicating with CIC staff (Citizenship and Immigration Canada), the candidate for citizenship must also pass the citizenship test which is usually written (multiple choice questions). The test has questions about Canada and the rights and responsibilities of Canadian citizenship, history and geography.

All the questions in this book are derived from the study guide "Discover Canada: The Rights and Responsibilities of Citizenship" which is excellent and is provided free by Citizenship and Immigration Canada as the primary official source for study.

This book is designed to help you remember the facts in that study guide. We suggest that you use this book together with the study guide so that you will learn enough to not only easily pass the citizenship test, but also become a more knowledgeable citizen of Canada.

Full information on Canadian citizenship and immigration, and the free study guide may be obtained from the CIC official site:

Citizenship and Immigration Canada   **Citoyenneté et Immigration Canada**

www.cic.gc.ca

HOW TO USE THIS BOOK

As we stated before, this book is designed to help you remember the content of the official study guide. Because of this, we suggest that you use this book together with the study guide so that you will learn enough to not only easily pass the citizenship test, but also become a more knowledgeable citizen of Canada.

To accomplish this goal, much of the information in "Discover Canada: The Rights and Responsibilities of Citizenship," has been reduced to a series of simple questions, such as the following:

1. True/False Question

We swear (or affirm) true allegiance to the flag.	1

For every question, you will find the question on one page and the answer on the following page:

1. True/False Answer

1	False We swear (or affirm) true allegiance to <u>Her Majesty Queen Elizabeth the Second, Queen of Canada</u>.

Later in the book, the same question is repeated in three other formats:

2. Fill-in Question

We swear (or affirm) true allegiance to _____.

120

2. Fill-in Answer

120 **Her Majesty Queen Elizabeth the Second, Queen of Canada.**
We swear (or affirm) true allegiance to <u>Her Majesty Queen Elizabeth the Second, Queen of Canada</u>.

3. A/B Multiple Choice Question

We swear (or affirm) true allegiance to:

A. Canada's flag
B. Her Majesty Queen Elizabeth the Second, Queen of Canada

240

3. A/B Multiple Choice Answer

240 | **B. Her Majesty Queen Elizabeth the Second, Queen of Canada**

We swear (or affirm) true allegiance to <u>Her Majesty Queen Elizabeth the Second, Queen of Canada</u>.

4. A/B/C/D Multiple Choice Question

We swear (or affirm) true allegiance to:

A. the constitution
B. the flag
C. Canada
D. Her Majesty Queen Elizabeth the Second, Queen of Canada

360

4. A/B/C/D Multiple Choice Answer

360 | D. Her Majesty Queen Elizabeth the Second, Queen of Canada

In addition to providing increasing levels of difficulty, many questions are designed to help you remember other important information by providing that information as part of the answer to the question.

Easy enough? YES! -*LET'S START ON THE ROAD TO SUCCESS!*

TRUE OR FALSE? (Answers are on the next page.)

We swear (or affirm) true allegiance to the flag.	1
Our sovereign personifies Canada.	2
Immigrants and settlers have been coming to Canada for 500 years.	3
Canada is a federal state and a parliamentary democracy.	4
To become a Canadian citizen, a person between the ages of 18 and 54 must have adequate knowledge of both French and English.	5
For an applicant not to be required to write the citizenship test, the applicant must be at least 62 years old.	6
A Notice to Appear to Take the Oath of Citizenship is given to a citizenship applicant as soon as the application is filed.	7
At the Oath of Citizenship Ceremony, the applicant takes the Oath of Citizenship.	8

ANSWERS

1	**False** We swear (or affirm) true allegiance to <u>Her Majesty Queen Elizabeth the Second, Queen of Canada</u>.
2	**True** Our sovereign is Her Majesty Queen Elizabeth the Second, Queen of Canada.
3	**False** Immigrants and settlers have been coming to Canada for <u>400</u> years.
4	**True** Canada is also a constitutional monarchy.
5	**False** To become a Canadian citizen, a person must learn the history of Canada and must converse in English <u>OR</u> French.
6	**False** An applicant has to be at least <u>55 years</u> old to not be required to write the citizenship test.
7	**False** A Notice to Appear to Take the Oath of Citizenship is given to a citizenship applicant <u>AFTER</u> the applicant passes the test.
8	**True** At the Oath of Citizenship Ceremony, the applicant takes the Oath of Citizenship.

TRUE OR FALSE?

If an applicant does not pass the Citizenship Test, the applicant cannot take the test again.	9
At the ceremony, an applicant for citizenship must pay a citizenship fee.	10
A source of Canadian law is the laws enacted by the North Atlantic Treaty Organization.	11
The Magna Carta, signed in 1215, is also known as the Constitution.	12
The Magna Carta ensures freedom from jail and paying taxes.	13
One of the rights included in the Magna Carta is the right to get rich.	14
A legal procedure designed to challenge the unlawful detention of a person by the state is known as a subpoena.	15
In 1982 the Canadian Constitution was amended to include the Liberties Manifesto.	16

ANSWERS

9	**False** **If an applicant does not pass the Citizenship Test, the applicant receives a notice regarding the next steps.**
10	**False: At the ceremony, an applicant for citizenship:** **1. takes the Oath of Citizenship.** **2. signs a form called the "oath form," and** **3. is given the Canadian Citizenship Certificate.**
11	**False** **Sources of Canadian law are: 1) the civil code of France and 2) English common law and 3) laws passed by the provincial legislatures and parliament 3. Great Britain's unwritten constitution**
12	**False** **The Magna Carta, signed in 1215, is also known as the <u>Great Charter of Freedoms</u>.**
13	**False** **The Magna Carta ensures freedom of conscience and religion**
14	**False. The following rights are included in the Magna Carta: Freedom of conscience and religion; Freedom of peaceful assembly; Freedom of thought, belief, opinion and expression, including freedom of speech and of the press; Freedom of association.**
15	**False: habeas corpus** **A legal procedure designed to challenge the unlawful detention of a person by the state is known as <u>habeas corpus</u>.**
16	**False: Canadian Charter of Rights and Freedoms.** **In 1982 the Canadian Constitution was amended to include the <u>Canadian Charter of Rights and Freedoms</u>.**

TRUE OR FALSE?

The words "Whereas Canada is founded upon principles that recognize the supremacy of God and the rule of law-" are the first words in the Magna Carta.	17
The Canadian Charter of Rights and Freedoms begins with "Whereas Canada is founded upon principles that recognize the supremacy of God and the rule of law."	18
The Habeas Corpus Act summarizes fundamental freedoms, including Official Language Rights and Minority Language Educational Rights.	19
Men and women in Canada have different rights under the law.	20
The following are Citizenship responsibilities: obeying the law, serving on a jury, and voting in elections.	21
In Canada military service is compulsory.	22
Canadian Aboriginal peoples migrated from Asia in the 1800's.	23
The three groups referred to with the term Aboriginal Peoples are Comanche, Aztec and Huron.	24

ANSWERS

17	**False** The words "Whereas Canada is founded upon principles that recognize the supremacy of God and the rule of law-" are the first words in the <u>Constitution of Canada</u>.
18	**True** The Canadian Charter of Rights and Freedoms was entrenched in the Constitution of Canada in the year 1982.
19	**False:** The <u>Canadian Charter of Rights and Freedoms</u> summarizes fundamental freedoms, including Official Language Rights and Minority Language Educational Rights. (also Mobility Rights, Aboriginal Peoples' Rights, and Multiculturalism.)
20	**False** Men and women in Canada have the same rights under the law. Persons who are guilty of crimes such as "honour killings" and other similar criminal acts are punished by Canadian law.
21	**True** Other citizenship responsibilities include taking responsibility for oneself and one's family, helping others in the community and protecting and enjoying our heritage and environment.
22	**False** In Canada military service is <u>NOT</u> compulsory. Serving in the Canadian Forces or helping in the community is voluntary.
23	**False:** Canadian Aboriginal peoples migrated from Asia <u>thousands of years ago</u>. The Constitution contains aboriginal and treaty rights. (King George III made the Royal Proclamation of 1763 which stated the basis for negotiating treaties between aboriginals and newcomers.)
24	**False:** The three groups referred to as Aboriginal Peoples are <u>Indian (First Nations), Inuit and Métis</u>. (From about 1800 – 1980, children of aboriginal peoples were forced to be educated in residential schools. This led to some abuses and the schools were not successful.)

TRUE OR FALSE?

John Buchan said that immigrant groups, "should retain their individuality and each make its contribution to the national character."	25
Some Nations people live in about 600 communities in Quebec.	26
The name "Inuit" means "the people." The Inuit speak the Inuktitut language and live in the arctic region.	27
The people that are comprised of Aboriginal and European ancestry are called Inuit.	28
The Métis make up about 30% of the Aboriginal peoples.	29
The two official languages of Canada are English and Spanish.	30
In 1604 French colonists started settling in the Maritime provinces. The descendants of these settlers are called Aboriginals.	31
People of Quebec are called Quebecers. Most speak French, but about one million Anglo-Quebecers speak Spanish.	32

ANSWERS

25	**True** John Buchan, 1st Baron Tweedsmuir and Governor General of Canada from 1935 – 1940.
26	**False** Some Nations people live in about 600 communities <u>on reserve</u> land. Others live <u>off-reserve</u>, usually in urban areas.
27	**True** The arctic is a harsh environment. In order to live there, the Inuit have accumulated great knowledge about the wildlife and land of the arctic.
28	**False: The people that are comprised of Aboriginal and European ancestry are called <u>Métis</u>.** The Métis have both English speaking and French speaking backgrounds, but also speak their own Michif dialect.
29	**True** First Nations (65%), Métis (30%), Inuit (4%) Aboriginal peoples are those whose ancestors migrated to Canada from Asia thousands of years ago.
30	**False: The two main languages of Canada are English and French.** (18 million English speaking "Anglophones" and 7 million speaking "Francophones") Most French speaking people reside in the province of Quebec.
31	**False: In 1604 French colonists started settling in Maritime provinces.** The descendants of these settlers are called <u>Acadians</u>. Two thirds of Acadians were deported from their living area between 1755 and 1763 (during the "Great Upheaval" – during the Britain/French war).
32	**False: People of Quebec are called Quebecers. Most speak French, but about one million Anglo-Quebecers speak <u>English</u>.** Anglo-Quebecers are descendants of Irish, Welsh, Scottish and English settlers. They are usually called English Canadians.

TRUE OR FALSE?

Most immigrants to Canada (since 1970) are from Europe.	33
In two of the largest cities of Canada, English is the most widely spoken language at home, followed by the non official language of Greek.	34
The first Europeans that explored Canada called the native people "Indians" because they believed that they were in the East Indies.	35
After Aboriginals came into contact with Europeans, many died of diseases because they lacked immunity.	36
The name of the people that colonized Greenland (1,000 years ago) and also set foot on Newfoundland and Labrador is Vikings.	37
The name Canada comes from an Iroquoian (Indian) word "kanata," which means country.	38
In 1604 European settlements were established in 1604 by explorers Pierre de Monts and Samuel de Champlain, both French.	39
Samuel de Champlain made an alliance with the Apaches Indians.	40

ANSWERS

33	Most immigrants (since 1970) come from <u>Asia</u>. Because of Canada's immigration, Canada is spoken of as being the "land of immigrants."
34	False In two of the largest cities of Canada, English is the most widely spoken language at home, followed by the non official languages of <u>Chinese</u>.
35	True Some Indians were hunters, farmers, nomadic and some were hunter-gatherers.
36	True In spite of this, in the first 200 years of Canada's history, there existed economic and military bonds between the Aboriginals and the settlers.
37	True Also, in 1497 John Cabot (Italian immigrant to England) drew a map of Canada's east coast. Also, Jacques Cartier (French) between 1534 and 1542 claimed the land for the King of France, King Francis I.
38	False The name Canada comes from an Iroquoian (Indian tribe) word "kanata", which means <u>village</u>. The name "Canada" first appeared on maps.
39	True: European settlements were established in 1604 by explorers Pierre de Monts and Samuel de Champlain, both French. The settlements were established on St. Croix Island and Port-Royal. (St. Croix Island is in Maine (US) and at Port-Royal in Acadia (Canada).
40	False: Samuel de Champlain made an alliance with <u>the Huron, Montagnais and Algonquin.</u> The Iroquois and the French battled for almost a century. They made peace in the year 1701. (The Iroquois were enemies with the Huron, Montagnais and Algonquin.)

TRUE OR FALSE?

The company that King Charles II (1670) granted exclusive trading rights in the Hudson Bay area was Furs of Canada Company.	41
The British defeated the French in 1759 in a battle called the Battle of the Plains of Abraham at Quebec City. This defeat marked the end of the French Empire in America.	42
The people living in the "Province of Quebec" under the English speaking British Empire are known as "habitants" or "Canadiens."	43
Around 1776 people loyal to the Crown fled the thirteen American colonies and settled in Nova Scotia and Quebec. These people were called Loyalists.	44
The Act of 1791 which divided the Province of Quebec into Upper Canada (present day Ontario) and Lower Canada (present day Quebec) is known as The Constitutional Act of 1791.	45
Slavery was abolished first in the province of Upper Canada in 1793. Its first Lieutenant Governor was Lieutenant Colonel John Graves Simcoe. He founded the City of York whose present day name is Toronto.	46
Mary Ann (Shadd) Carey, the first woman publisher in Canada, in 1853 founded and edited the Provincial Freeman, which encouraged separation from British rule.	47
In the 1800's Canadian financial institutions began to emerge. In 1832 the Montreal Stock exchange was opened.	48

ANSWERS

41	**False** **The company that King Charles II (1670) granted exclusive trading rights in the Hudson Bay area was <u>Hudson's Bay Company.</u>**
42	**True: The British defeated the French in 1759 in a battle called the Battle of the Plains of Abraham at Quebec City. <u>This defeat marked the end of the French Empire in America</u>. Brigadier James Wolfe led the British and the Marquis de Montcalm led the French. They were both killed in the battle.**
43	**True: The people living in the "Province of Quebec" under the English speaking British Empire are known as "habitants" or "Canadiens." The British Parliament passed the "Quebec Act of 1774." This act permitted the French speaking Catholic people to hold public office.**
44	**True** **Some of the black Loyalists (freed slaves) settled in Nova Scotia. In 1792 some moved to Africa and established Freetown in Sierra Leone (West Africa).**
45	**True: The Act of 1791 which divided the Province of Quebec into Upper Canada (present day Ontario) and Lower Canada (present day Quebec) is known as The Constitutional Act of 1791. Upper Canada was mainly English speaking and Lower Canada was mainly French speaking.**
46	**True: Slavery was abolished in the province of Upper Canada (1793). Its first Lieutenant Governor was Lieutenant Colonel John Graves Simcoe. He founded the City of York (present day Toronto). In 1807 the buying and selling of slaves was abolished by the British Parliament.**
47	**False: Mary Ann (Shadd) Carey, the first woman publisher in Canada, in 1853 founded and edited the Provincial Freeman, which encouraged <u>anti-slavery and black immigration to Canada</u>. She also encouraged the support of British rule and drinking less alcohol.**
48	**True: In the 1800's Canadian financial institutions began to emerge. In 1832 the Montreal Stock exchange was opened.** **Before the 1800's the economy of Canada relied mostly on its natural resources (fish, timber, furs, etc.) and on farming.**

TRUE OR FALSE?

The USA invaded Canada in the year 1776.	**49**
The rebellion of 1837-38 occurred mainly because some people thought that democracy was not coming fast enough to Canada.	50
The person who suggested that Lower Canada and Upper Canada be merged and given "responsible government" was John Cabot.	**51**
The Province of Canada was the result of the 1840 unification of Upper and Lower Canada.	52
The Dominion of Canada was established by the Fathers of Confederation in 1867.	**53**
On July 1, 1867 the Fathers of Confederation established Canada. July 1 was celebrated as "Dominion Day" until 1982. However, today "Dominion Day" is called Veterans Day.	54
Ontario, Quebec, Nova Scotia, New Brunswick joined Canada in 1867.	**55**
Canada's first Prime Minister (1867) was Sir Sam Steele.	56

ANSWERS

49	**False: USA invaded Canada in 1813 (during War of 1812). In 1813 Americans burned government buildings in present day Toronto. The border between the U.S. and Canada is one of the results of the War of 1812.**
50	**True: The rebellion of 1837-38 occurred mainly because some people thought that democracy was not coming fast enough to Canada. Also, some Canadians were in favor of joining the United States.**
51	**False: It was <u>Lord Durham</u>. "Responsible government" that Lord Durham recommended meant that British ministers to govern needed the support of the majority of the elected representatives of the Canadian people.**
52	**True The Province of Canada was the result of the 1840 unification of Upper and Lower Canada. In 1848-49 "responsible government" was introduced in Canada by Lord Elgin, governor of United Canada.**
53	**True The Dominion of Canada was established by the Fathers of Confederation in 1867. Two levels of government (federal and provincial) were introduced.**
54	**False: On July 1, 1867 the Fathers of Confederation established Canada. July 1 was celebrated as "Dominion Day" until 1982. Today it is called <u>Canada Day</u>. The term "Dominion of Canada" was suggested by Sir Leonard Tilley, one of the Fathers of Confederation, in 1864.**
55	**True: (1867) Ontario, Quebec, Nova Scotia, New Brunswick; (1870) Manitoba, Northwest Territories (N.W.T.); (1871) British Columbia; (1873) Prince Edward Island; (1880) Transfer of Arctic Islands to N.W.T; (1898) Yukon Territory; (1905) Saskatchewan, Alberta; (1949) Newfoundland and Labrador; (1999) Nnavut**
56	**False Canada's first Prime Minister (1867) was <u>Sir John Alexander Macdonald</u>. Sir John Alexander Macdonald's portrait is on the $10 bill. On January 11 we celebrate Sir John A. Macdonald Day.**

TRUE OR FALSE?

Sir George-Étienne Cartier, a patriotic Canadien, this person was from Quebec and an architect of Confederation.	57
Prime Minister Macdonald in 1873 established the NWMP (North West Mounted Police).	58
The first French-Canadian prime minister, Sir Wilfrid Laurier, is on the $10 bill.	59
The person known as "Canada's greatest soldier" is Sir Arthur Currie.	60
The founder of the woman's suffrage movement in Canada was Nancy Baker.	61
Remembrance Day is observed on January 21.	62
The British Commonwealth of Nations is a free association of states.	63
In the D-Day battle of WWII, one in ten of the Allied soldiers was Canadian.	64

ANSWERS

57	True: <u>Sir George-Étienne Cartier</u> , who also was instrumental in the negotiations for the following territories to enter into Canada: Manitoba, Northwest Territories, and British Columbia.
58	True: Prime Minister Macdonald in 1873 established the NWMP (North West Mounted Police), now the Royal Canadian Mounted Police, Canada's national police force. NWMP were established after the first Métis uprising.
59	False: First French-Canadian prime minister since confederation, Sir Wilfrid Laurier, is on the $5 bill. He encouraged people to immigrate to the West. Immigration was also helped by the railway from Sea to Sea, completed in 1885, built mostly by European and Chinese labour.
60	True: The person known as "Canada's greatest soldier" is Sir Arthur Currie. He fought in WWI. Canadian troops volunteered to fight in a number of wars, including the South African War (1899-1902).
61	False: The founder of the woman's suffrage movement in Canada was Dr. Emily Stowe. Nurses were granted the right to vote in 1917 and most Canadian female citizens over 21 in 1918.
62	False: Remembrance Day is <u>November 11</u>. We remember the 110,000 Canadians who gave their lives in wars by wearing the red poppy and observing a moment of silence. "In Flanders Fields," composed by Lt. Col. John McCrae in 1915, is recited on Remembrance Day.
63	True: The British Commonwealth of Nations is a free association of states. It includes Canada, Australia, India, some African countries and some Caribbean countries.
64	True: In the D-Day battle of WWII, one in ten of the Allied soldiers was Canadian. In the second World War (1939-1945), more than one million Canadians served in the armed forces.

TRUE OR FALSE?

The Act which guarantees health insurance coverage to Canadians is The Suffrage Act.	65
The Act which guarantees French language rights and services in all of Canada is The Official Languages Act (1969).	66
The "Group of Seven" (founded in 1920) developed a style of painting.	67
The sport of basketball was invented by Donovan Bailey in 1886.	68
The Canadian who invented the worldwide system of standard time zones was Sir Sandford Fleming.	69
The British North America Act of 1867 (known now as the Constitution Act of 1867) defined the responsibilities of the provincial and federal governments of Canada.	70
Canada's type of government is a parliamentary democracy.	71
The three parts of Parliament are: the Senate, and House of Commons, and the Sovereign.	72

ANSWERS

65	**False: The Act which guarantees health insurance coverage is <u>The Canada Health Act.</u> Unemployment insurance was introduced in 1940 by the Canadian government. Education is provided by the provinces and territories.**
66	**True: The Act which guarantees French language rights and services in all of Canada is <u>The Official Languages Act (1969)</u>.**
67	**True** **The "Group of Seven" (founded in 1920) developed a style of painting.**
68	**False: The sport of basketball was invented by <u>James Naismith in 1891</u>. Sports in Canada are popular in all provinces.** **Canadian scientists have contributed greatly to the world.**
69	**True: The Canadian who invented the worldwide system of standard time zones was <u>Sir Sandford Fleming</u>. (Reginald Fassenden contributed to the invention of the radio. Dr. John A. Hopps invented the pacemaker).**
70	**True: The British North America Act of 1867 (known now as the Constitution Act of 1867) defined the responsibilities of the provincial and federal governments of Canada.** **Each province has a Legislative Assembly which it elects.**
71	**True** **Canada's type of government is a <u>parliamentary democracy</u>.** **If the Cabinet ministers receive a "no-confidence" vote, they must resign.**
72	**True: The three parts of Parliament are: the Senate, and House of Commons, and the Sovereign. The provinces have legislatures that are comprised of the elected Assembly and the Governor of the province.**

TRUE OR FALSE?

In the federal government, the Prime Minister appoints Cabinet members and has responsibility for government policy and operations.	73
When a bill is considered read for the first time and is printed, it is at step 1, called the "Report Stage".	74
Members debate and vote on a bill in the Report Stage.	75
The minimum age at which Canadians can vote is 14.	76
In Canada the head of state is the Sovereign. The head of government is the Prime Minister.	77
The three branches of government are the Executive, Legislative and Judicial.	78
Members of the House of Parliament are also called MPs (or Members of Parliament).	79
The MP (Member of Parliament) is chosen by the voters in an electoral district.	80

ANSWERS

73	**True: In the federal government, the Prime Minister selects Cabinet members and has responsibility for government policy and operations. House of Commons is elected by the people every 4 years. Senators are appointed by the Prime Minister. Laws are passed by both chambers and royal assent.**
74	**False: When a bill is considered read for the first time and is printed, it is at step 1, called the <u>First Reading</u>. There are 7 steps in a bill becoming law: 1) First Reading, 2) Second Reading, 3) Committee Stage, 4) Report Stage, 5) Third Reading, 6) Senate, 7) Royal Assent.**
75	**True: Members debate and vote on a bill in the <u>Report Stage</u>. There are 7 steps in a bill becoming law: 1) First Reading, 2) Second Reading, 3) Committee Stage, 4) Report Stage, 5) Third Reading, 6) Senate, 7) Royal Assent.**
76	**False: The minimum age at which Canadians can vote is <u>18</u>. Canada is a Constitutional Monarchy. Canada's Head of State is the Sovereign The Commonwealth has 52 member states.**
77	**True: In Canada the head of state is the Sovereign. The head of government is the Prime Minister. The Governor General represents the Sovereign. Each of the 10 provinces has a Lieutenant Governor (appointed by the Governor General on advice of the Prime Minister).**
78	**True: The three branches of government are the Executive, Legislative and Judicial. The Premier (of each province) is similar to the Prime Minister.**
79	**True: Members of the House of Parliament are also called MPs (or Members of Parliament). Federal elections are held every 4 years (in October) following the most recent general election. The prime Minister can ask the Governor General to call an election sooner.**
80	**True: The MP (Member of Parliament) is chosen by the voters in an electoral district. Canada has 308 electoral districts (also called constituencies or "ridings"). MPs sit in the House of Commons. The minimum age to run in a federal election is 18.**

TRUE OR FALSE?

Elections Canada, an agency of parliament, produces a list of eligible voters called the <u>National Register of Electors</u>.	**81**
The party with the most seats in the House of Commons forms the government (after being invited to do so by the Governor General). If that party holds half the seats or more in the House of Commons, the government it forms is called the majority government.	**82**
The Cabinet is made up of the Prime Minister and the Assemblymen.	**83**
The House of Commons presently has members of four major political parties: the Liberal Party, the New Democratic Party, the Bloc Quebecois, and the Populist Party.	**84**
On a voting ballot, you mark an X to indicate the name of the candidate that you wish to vote for.	**85**
Laws passed by local or municipal governments are called "by-laws."	**86**
Presumption of innocence (everyone is innocent until proven guilty) is the foundation of the Canadian judicial system.	**87**
The highest court in Canada is the Supreme Court of Canada.	**88**

ANSWERS

81	**True: Elections Canada, an agency of parliament produces a list called the National Register of Electors. To vote in a federal election, a person must: 1. be a Canadian citizen, 2. be at least 18 (on voting day), 3. be on the National Register of Electors.**
82	**True: The party with most seats in the House of Commons forms the government. If that party holds half the seats or more in the House of Commons, the government it forms is called the majority government. (If it holds less than half the seats, it is called the minority government.).**
83	**False: The Cabinet is made up of the Prime Minister and Cabinet ministers. The Cabinet makes decisions on running the country. These decisions may be questioned by the Official Opposition (Opposing party with the most members) and by parties not in power.**
84	**False: The House of Commons presently has members of four major political parties: the Liberal Party, the New Democratic Party, the Bloc Quebecois, and the Conservative Party.**
85	**True** **On a voting ballot, you mark an X to indicate the name of the candidate that you wish to vote for.**
86	**True: Laws passed by local or municipal governments are called "by-laws." Municipal and local governments have responsibilities in: policing, firefighting, emergency services, recycling programs, transportation, community affairs, community health and utilities.**
87	**True: Presumption of innocence (everyone is innocent until proven guilty) is the foundation of the Canadian judicial system. Courts settle disputes. Police enforce laws. Due process means that all the legal rights of a person must be respected by the government.**
88	**True** **The highest court in Canada is the Supreme Court of Canada. (Provinces have a number of lesser courts.)**

TRUE OR FALSE?

The Royal Canadian Mounted Police (RCMP) enforce federal Canadian laws and are the provincial police in all territories and provinces, except the provinces of Quebec and Ontario.	**89**
The Crown is a symbol of government, the courts, the police services, the armed forces, and the legislatures.	**90**
National Flag day is February 15.	**91**
The most popular spectator sport in Canada is ice hockey.	**92**
The animal that is on the five cent coin is a pigeon.	**93**
The National anthem of Canada is "O Canada."	**94**
The highest honour that a Canadian can receive is The Victoria Cross (V.C.).	**95**
Sir John A. Macdonald Day is celebrated on January 11.	**96**

ANSWERS

89	**True** The Royal Canadian Mounted police (RCMP) Canadian enforce federal laws and are the provincial police in all territories and provinces, except the provinces of Quebec and Ontario.
90	**True** The Crown is a symbol of government, the courts, the police services, the armed forces, and the legislatures.
91	**True: National Flag day is February 15 (Canadian flag was first raised on February 15, 1965). It has a red-white-red pattern. The Maple leaf is also a Canadian symbol. The coat of arms and "A Mari Usque Ad Mare" ("from Sea to Sea") are used on currency, public buildings, government documents.**
92	**True: The most popular spectator sport in Canada is ice hockey.** **The second most popular sport is Canadian football.** **The sport with the most registered players is soccer.**
93	**False** The animal that is on the five cent coin is the <u>beaver</u>.
94	**True: The National anthem of Canada is "O Canada."** **(The "Royal Anthem" is sung whenever the Queen is honored.)** **Citizens worthy of recognition are awarded the "Order of Canada."**
95	**True** The highest honour that a Canadian can receive is <u>The Victoria Cross (V.C.)</u>.
96	**True: Sir John A. Macdonald Day is celebrated on January 11.** **Vimy Day – April 9** **Victoria Day – Monday preceding May 25 (Sovereign birthday)** **Fete Nationale (Quebec) June 24 (Feast of St. John the Baptist)**

TRUE OR FALSE?

Remembrance Day is celebrated NOVEMBER 11.	97
Today more than 75% of Canadians work in Service industries.	98
The biggest trading partner of Canada is the U.S.A.	99
The second largest country in the world is Canada.	100
Canada has 5 distinct regions.	101
The national capital of Canada is Ottawa.	102
Canada has 3 provinces.	103
The population of Canada is 33 million (2010).	104

ANSWERS

97	**True: Remembrance Day is celebrated NOVEMBER 11** **Also remember:** **Sir Wilfrid Laurier Day – November 20** **Christmas – December 25**
98	**True** **Today more than 75% of Canadians work in Service industries.**
99	**True** **The biggest trading partner of Canada is the U.S.A.** **The U.S.A./Canadian border is the world's longest undefended border.**
100	**True** **The second largest country in the world is Canada.** **Canada is bordered by the Atlantic Ocean, Pacific Ocean and the U.S.A.**
101	**True: Canada has 5 distinct regions: 1. The Atlantic Provinces, 2. The Prairie Provinces, 3. The Northern Territories, 4. Ontario and Quebec, 5. The West Coast.**
102	**True** **The national capital of Canada is Ottawa.** **(In 1857 Queen Victoria selected Ottawa as the capital.)**
103	**False: Canada has 10 provinces.** **Canada has 10 provinces and 3 territories.** **(Memorize the capitals of your province or territory and the capital of Canada.)**
104	**True** **Most Canadians live in cities.**

TRUE OR FALSE?

The capital of Nova Scotia is Halifax.	105
The capital of Ontario is Toronto.	106
Newfoundland and Labrador is the oldest colony and the province with the most easterly point in North America. It is also known for its fisheries.	107
The only officially bilingual province is New Brunswick.	108
The largest city in Canada is Toronto. It is located in the province of Ontario.	109
The two provinces known as the Prairie Provinces are Manitoba and Saskatchewan.	110
The Prairie Province that is most populous is Alberta.	111
The Port of Vancouver is found in the Province of British Columbia.	112

ANSWERS

105	**True** **Also memorize:** **Newfoundland and Labrador – capital is St. John's** **New Brunswick – capital is Fredericton**
106	**True: The capital of Ontario is Toronto. Also remember: Quebec – Quebec City...Manitoba – Winnipeg...Saskatchewan – Regina...Alberta – Edmonton...British Columbia – Victoria...Nanavut – Igaluit...Northwest Territories – Yellowknife...Yukon Territory - Whitehorse**
107	**True: Newfoundland and Labrador is the oldest colony and province with most easterly point in North America; also known for its fisheries. The smallest province is Prince Edward Island. The Atlantic province with the most population is Nova Scotia.**
108	**True: The only officially bilingual province is New Brunswick.** **Most people in Canada (more than half) live in Ontario and Quebec. In Quebec three-quarters of the people speak French as their first language.**
109	**True** **The largest city in Canada is Toronto. It is located in the province of Ontario. Ontario has 12 million people and has the Niagara region.**
110	**True** **The two provinces known as the Prairie Provinces are Manitoba and Saskatchewan. Saskatchewan is known as the "breadbasket of the world" and the "wheat province."**
111	**True: The Prairie Province that is most populous is Alberta.** **The Province was named after Princess Louise Caroline Alberta, the fourth daughter of Queen Victoria.**
112	**True** **The Port of Vancouver is found in the Province of British Columbia. Chinese and Punjabi are spoken often in the cities, next to English.**

FILL-IN QUESTIONS

We swear (or affirm) true allegiance to _____.	**113**
The person who personifies Canada is _____ .	**114**
Immigrants and settlers have been coming to Canada for _____ years.	**115**
Canada is a federal state, a parliamentary democracy and _____.	**116**
To become a Canadian citizen, a person between the ages of 18 and 54 must have adequate knowledge of one of these two languages: _____ or _____.	**117**
To become a Canadian citizen, a person must learn about the history of _____.	**118**
For an applicant not to be required to write the citizenship test, the applicant must be at least ____ years old.	**119**
At the Oath of Citizenship Ceremony, the applicant _____.	**120**

ANSWERS

113	Her Majesty Queen Elizabeth the Second, Queen of Canada. We swear (or affirm) true allegiance to <u>Her Majesty Queen Elizabeth the Second, Queen of Canada</u>.
114	Her Majesty Queen Elizabeth the Second, Queen of Canada The person who personifies Canada is <u>Her Majesty Queen Elizabeth the Second, Queen of Canada.</u>
115	Immigrants and settlers have been coming to Canada for <u>400</u> years.
116	a constitutional monarchy Canada is a federal state, a parliamentary democracy and <u>a constitutional monarchy</u>.
117	English or French The person must also learn about the geography and democratic institutions of Canada, voting procedures, Canada's history, symbols, and responsibilities and rights of Canadian citizenship.
118	Canada A person must also learn about the geography of Canada.
119	55 For an applicant <u>not</u> to be required to write the citizenship test, the applicant must be at least <u>55</u> years old.
120	takes the Oath of Citizenship. At the Oath of Citizenship Ceremony, the applicant <u>takes the Oath of Citizenship</u>.

FILL-IN QUESTIONS

If an applicant does not pass the Citizenship Test, the applicant _____.	121
At the Oath of Citizenship ceremony, an applicant for citizenship _____. (3 things)	122
A source of Canadian law is _____.	123
The Magna Carta, signed in 1215, is also known as _____.	124
The Magna Carta ensures _____.	125
The following freedoms are included in the Magna Carta: Freedom of conscience and religion; Freedom of thought, belief, opinion and expression, including freedom of speech and of the press; Freedom of peaceful assembly; and _____.	126
A legal procedure designed to challenge the unlawful detention of a person by the state is known as _____.	127
In 1982 the Canadian Constitution was amended to include the _____.	128

FILL-IN ANSWERS

121	receives a notification indicating the next steps If an applicant does not pass the Citizenship Test, the applicant <u>receives a notice regarding the next steps.</u>
122	At the ceremony, an applicant for citizenship 1. takes the Oath of Citizenship, 2. signs a form called the "oath form," and 3. is given the Canadian Citizenship Certificate.
123	all the following: 1. the civil code of France, 2. English common law and laws passed by the provincial legislatures and parliament, 3. Great Britain's unwritten constitution
124	The Great Charter of Freedoms. The Magna Carta, signed in 1215, is also known as <u>The Great Charter of Freedoms.</u>
125	freedom of conscience and religion The Magna Carta ensures <u>freedom of conscience and religion.</u>
126	Freedom of association. The following freedoms are included: Freedom of conscience and religion; Freedom of thought, belief, opinion and expression, including freedom of speech and of the press; Freedom of peaceful assembly; and <u>Freedom of association</u>
127	habeas corpus. A legal procedure designed to challenge the unlawful detention of a person by the state is known as <u>habeas corpus.</u>
128	Canadian Charter of Rights and Freedoms. In 1982 the Canadian Constitution was amended to include <u>The Canadian Charter of Rights and Freedoms</u>.

FILL-IN QUESTIONS

The words, "Whereas Canada is founded upon principles that recognize the supremacy of God and the rule of law-" are the first words in the _____.	**129**
In addition to the Constitution of Canada, the _____ begins with "Whereas Canada is founded upon principles that recognize the supremacy of God and the rule of law."	**130**
The _____ summarizes fundamental freedoms, including Official Language Rights and Minority Language Educational Rights.	**131**
Men and women in Canada have _____ rights under the law.	**132**
Citizenship responsibilities include: obeying the law, serving on a jury, and _____. (4 additional things)	**133**
In Canada military service is not _____.	**134**
Canadian Aboriginal peoples migrated from Asia (when?) _____.	**135**
The three groups referred to with the term "Aboriginal Peoples" are _____.	**136**

FILL-IN ANSWERS

129	**Constitution of Canada.** The words "Whereas Canada is founded upon principles that recognize the supremacy of God and the rule of law-" are the first words in the <u>Constitution of Canada</u>.
130	**Canadian Charter of Rights and Freedoms** The <u>Canadian Charter of Rights and Freedoms</u> was entrenched in the Constitution of Canada in the year 1982.
131	**Canadian Charter of Rights and Freedoms.** The <u>Canadian Charter of Rights and Freedoms</u> summarizes fundamental freedoms, including Official Language Rights and Minority Language Educational Rights. (also Mobility Rights, Aboriginal Peoples' Rights, and Multiculturalism.)
132	**same (rights)** Persons who are guilty of crimes such as "honour killings" and other similar criminal acts are punished by Canadian law.
133	1. voting in elections 2. taking responsibility for oneself and one's family, 3. helping others in the community, and 4. protecting and enjoying our heritage and environment.
134	**compulsory** In Canada military service is <u>NOT compulsory</u>. Serving in the Canadian Forces or helping in the community is voluntary.
135	Canadian Aboriginals migrated from Asia <u>thousands of years ago</u>. The Canadian Constitution contains aboriginal and treaty rights. King George III made the Royal Proclamation of 1763, stating the basis for negotiating treaties between aboriginals and newcomers.
136	**Indian (First Nations), Inuit and Métis.** (From about 1800 – 1980, children of aboriginal peoples were forced to be educated in residential schools. This led to some abuses and the schools were not successful.)

FILL-IN QUESTIONS

_____ said that immigrant groups, "should retain their individuality and each make its contribution to the national character" and that immigrant groups could learn "from the other...."	**137**
Some Nations people live in about 600 communities (where?) _____.	**138**
The name _____ means "the people." They speak the Inuktitut language and live in the arctic region.	**139**
The people that are comprised of Aboriginal and European ancestry are called _____.	**140**
The Métis make up about ___% of the Aboriginal peoples.	**141**
The two official languages of Canada are _____.	**142**
In 1604 French colonists started settling in the Maritime provinces. The descendants of these settlers are called _____.	**143**
People of Quebec are called Quebecers. Most speak French, but about one million Anglo-Quebecers speak _____.	**144**

FILL-IN ANSWERS

137	**John Buchan, 1st Baron Tweedsmuir and Governor General of Canada** from 1935 – 1940. He also said that "while they cherish their own special loyalties and traditions, they cherish not less that new loyalty and tradition which springs from their union."
138	**on reserve land** Some Nations people live in about 600 communities **on reserve land**. Others live off-reserve, usually in urban areas.
139	**Inuit** The arctic is a harsh environment. In order to live there, the **Inuit** have accumulated great knowledge about the wildlife and land of the arctic.
140	**Métis** The people that are comprised of Aboriginal and European ancestry are called **Métis**. The Métis have both English speaking and French speaking backgrounds, but also speak their own Michif dialect.
141	**30%** First Nations (65%), Métis (30%), Inuit (4%) Aboriginal peoples are those whose ancestors migrated to Canada from Asia thousands of years in the past.
142	**English and French.** (18 million English speaking "Anglophones" and 7 million French speaking "Francophones.") Most French speaking people reside in the province of Quebec. One province (New Brunswick) is the only province that is officially bilingual.
143	**Acadians** Two thirds of Acadians were deported from their living area between 1755 and 1763 (during the "Great Upheaval" – during the Britain/French war).
144	**English.** People of Quebec are called Quebecers. Most speak French, but about one million Anglo-Quebecers speak **English**. Anglo-Quebecers are descendants of Irish, Welsh, Scottish and English settlers. They are usually called English Canadians.

FILL-IN QUESTIONS

Most recent immigrants to Canada (since 1970) come from _____. (continent)	145
In two of the largest cities of Canada, English is the most widely spoken language at home, followed by the non official languages of _____.	146
The first Europeans that explored Canada called the native people "Indians" because they believed that they were in the _____.	147
After Aboriginals came into contact with Europeans, many died of diseases to which they lacked _____.	148
The name of the people that colonized Greenland (1,000 years ago) and also set foot on Newfoundland and Labrador is _____.	149
The name Canada comes from an Iroquoian (Indian) word kanata, which means _____.	150
European settlements were established in 1604 by explorers Pierre de Monts and _____, both French.	151
Samuel de Champlain made an alliance with the _____ Indians (3 tribes).	152

FILL-IN ANSWERS

145	Asia. Recent immigrants (since 1970) are from Asia. Canada is spoken of as being the "land of immigrants." Most numerous people living in Canada are: English, French, Scottish, Irish, German, Italian, Chinese, Aboriginal, Ukranian, Dutch, South Asian, and Scandinavian.
146	Chinese In two of the largest cities of Canada, English is the most widely spoken language at home, followed by the non official languages of Chinese.
147	East Indies Some Indians were hunters, farmers, nomadic and some were hunter-gatherers.
148	immunity In spite of this, in the first 200 years of Canada's history, there developed economic and military bonds between the Aboriginals and the settlers.
149	Vikings Also, in 1497 John Cabot (Italian immigrant to England) drew a map of Canada's east coast. Also, Jacques Cartier (French) between 1534 and 1542 claimed the land for the King of France, King Francis I.
150	village The name Canada comes from an Iroquoian (Indian tribe) word "kanata", which means village. The name "Canada" first appeared on maps.
151	Samuel de Champlain. European settlements were established in 1604 by explorers Pierre de Monts and Samuel de Champlain, both French. The settlements were established on St. Croix Island and Port-Royal. (St. Croix Island is in Maine (US) and Port-Royal is in Acadia (Canada).
152	Huron, Montagnais and Algonquin. The Iroquois and the French battled for almost a century. They made peace in the year 1701. (The Iroquois were enemies with the Huron, Montagnais and Algonquin.)

FILL-IN QUESTIONS

The company that King Charles II (1670) granted exclusive trading rights in the Hudson Bay area was called _____.	153
The British defeated the French in _____ in the Battle of the Plains of Abraham at Quebec City. This ended the French Empire in America.	154
The people living in the "Province of Quebec" under the English speaking British Empire were known as _____.	155
Around 1776 people loyal to the Crown fled the thirteen American colonies and settled in Nova Scotia and Quebec. These people were called _____.	156
The Act in 1791 which divided the Province of Quebec into Upper Canada (present day Ontario) and Lower Canada (present day Quebec) is known as _____.	157
Slavery was abolished first in the province of Upper Canada in 1793. Its first Lieutenant Governor was Lieutenant Colonel John Graves Simcoe. He founded the City of York whose present day name is _____.	158
Mary Ann (Shadd) Carey, the first woman publisher in Canada, in 1853 founded and edited the Provincial Freeman, which encouraged _____.	159
In the 1800's Canadian financial institutions began to emerge. In 1832 the _____ Stock exchange was opened.	160

FILL-IN ANSWERS

153	Hudson's Bay Company. Furs were often collected by traders who often travelled by canoe. They formed agreements with the First Nations. These traders are referred to as "coureurs des bois" and "voyageurs".
154	The British defeated the French in <u>1759</u> in a battle called the Battle of the Plains of Abraham at Quebec City. This ended the French Empire in America. Brigadier James Wolfe led British soldiers and the Marquis de Montcalm led French soldiers. They were both killed in the battle.
155	People living in "Province of Quebec" were known as <u>habitants or Canadiens</u>. In 1774, the British Parliament passed the "Quebec Act of 1774" which permitted French speaking Catholic people to hold public office. It also established French civil law and English criminal law.
156	Loyalists Some of these black <u>Loyalists</u> (freed slaves) settled in Nova Scotia. In 1792 some moved to Africa and established Freetown in Sierra Leone (West Africa).
157	The Constitutional Act of 1791. Upper Canada was mainly English speaking and Lower Canada was mainly French speaking. "British North America" generally referred to the two Canadas (Upper and Lower) and the Atlantic colonies.
158	Toronto. In 1807 the buying and selling of slaves was abolished by the British Parliament, who also in 1833 abolished throughout the empire the buying and selling of slaves.
159	anti-slavery and black immigration to Canada. She also encouraged the support of British rule and drinking less alcohol.
160	Montreal. Before the 1800's the economy of Canada relied mostly on its natural resources (fish, timber, furs, etc.) and on farming.

FILL-IN QUESTIONS

The _____ invaded Canada in the year 1813.	**161**
The rebellion of _____ occurred mainly because some people thought that democracy was not coming fast enough to Canada.	**162**
The person who suggested that Lower Canada and Upper Canada be merged and given "responsible government" was _____.	**163**
The Province of Canada was the result of the 1840 unification of _____.	**164**
The Dominion of Canada was established by the _____ in 1867.	**165**
On July 1, 1867 the Fathers of Confederation established Canada. July 1 was celebrated as "Dominion Day" until 1982. However today "Dominion Day" is called _____.	**166**
Nanavut joined Canada in the year _____	**167**
Canada's first Prime Minister (1867) was _____.	**168**

FILL-IN ANSWERS

161	U.S.A. In 1813 Americans burned government buildings in present day Toronto. In 1814 the British burned the White House and other government buildings in Washington D.C. The border between the U.S. and Canada is one of the results of the War of 1812.
162	1837-38. The rebellion of 1837-38 occurred mainly because some people thought that British democracy was not coming fast enough to Canada. Also, some Canadians were in favor of joining the United States.
163	Lord Durham. "Responsible government," recommended by Lord Durham meant that ministers of the Crown needed the support of the majority of Canadian elected representatives. He mistakenly suggested that Canadiens needed to be assimilated into the English culture.
164	Upper and Lower Canada. "Responsible government" in the Province of Canada was advanced by reformers Robert Baldwin, Sir Louis-Hippolyte La Fontaine and Joseph Howe. In 1848-49 responsible government was introduced by Lord Elgin, governor of United Canada.
165	Fathers of Confederation The Dominion of Canada was established by the Fathers of Confederation in 1867. Two levels of government (federal and provincial) were introduced.
166	Canada Day. The term "Dominion of Canada" was suggested by Sir Leonard Tilley, one of the Fathers of Confederation, in the year 1864.
167	1999. (1867) Ontario, Quebec, Nova Scotia, New Brunswick; (1870) Manitoba, Northwest Territories (N.W.T.); (1871) British Columbia; (1873) Prince Edward Island ; (1880) Transfer of Arctic Islands to N.W.T; (1898) Yukon Territory; (1905) Saskatchewan, Alberta; (1949) Newfoundland and Labrador
168	Sir John Alexander Macdonald. Canada's first Prime Minister (1867) was Sir John Alexander Macdonald. Sir John Alexander Macdonald's portrait is on the $10 bill. On January 11 we celebrate Sir John A. Macdonald Day.

FILL-IN QUESTIONS

A patriotic Canadien, this person was from Quebec and a key architect of Confederation: _____.	169
Prime Minister Macdonald in 1873 established the _____.	170
The first French-Canadian prime minister since confederation, Sir Wilfrid Laurier, is on the ____ bill.	171
The person known as "Canada's greatest soldier" is _____.	172
The founder of the woman's suffrage movement in Canada was _____.	173
Remembrance Day is observed on _____.	174
The British Commonwealth of Nations is a free association of _____.	175
In the _____ battle of WWII, one in ten of the Allied soldiers was Canadian.	176

FILL-IN ANSWERS

169	Sir George-Étienne Cartier. He also was instrumental in the negotiations for the following territories to enter into Canada: Manitoba, Northwest Territories, and British Columbia.
170	Prime Minister Macdonald in 1873 established the NWMP (North West Mounted Police). The NWMP were established after the first Métis uprising. Two great Métis leaders were Louis Riel (father of Manitoba) and Gabriel Dumont.
171	$5 bill. Sir Wilfrid Laurier encouraged people to immigrate to the West. Immigration was also helped by the railway from Sea to Sea, completed in 1885. It was built mostly by European and Chinese labour.
172	The person known as "Canada's greatest soldier" is Sir Arthur Currie. Sir Arthur Currie fought in WWI. Canadian troops volunteered to fight in a number of wars, including the South African War (1899-1902).
173	Dr. Emily Stowe Nurses were granted the right to vote in 1917 and most Canadian female citizens over 21 in 1918.
174	Remembrance Day is on November 11, when we remember the sacrifice of 110,000 Canadians who gave their lives in wars. We wear the red poppy and observe a moment of silence. "In Flanders Fields," a poem composed by Lt. Col. John McCrae in 1915 is recited on this day.
175	The British Commonwealth of Nations is a free association of states. It includes Canada, Australia, India, some African countries and some Caribbean countries.
176	In the D-Day battle of WWII, one in ten Allied soldiers was Canadian. In the second World War (1939-1945), more than one million Canadians served in the armed forces.

FILL-IN QUESTIONS

The Act which guarantees health insurance coverage to Canadians is _____.	177
The Act which guarantees French language rights and services in all of Canada is the _____.	178
The "Group of Seven" (founded in 1920) developed a _____.	179
The sport of basketball was invented by _____ in 1891.	180
The Canadian who invented the worldwide system of standard time zones was _____.	181
The British North America Act of 1867 (known now as the Constitution Act of 1867) defined _____.	182
Canada's type of government is _____.	183
The three parts of Parliament are: the Senate, the House of Commons, and _____.	184

FILL-IN ANSWERS

177	The Act which guarantees health insurance coverage is <u>The Canada Health Act</u>. Unemployment insurance was introduced in 1940 by the Canadian government. Education is provided by the provinces and territories.
178	The Act which guarantees French language rights and services in all of Canada is <u>The Official Languages Act (1969)</u>.
179	The "Group of Seven" (founded in 1920) developed a <u>style of painting.</u>
180	The sport of basketball was invented by <u>James Naismith</u> in 1891. Sports in Canada are popular in all provinces. Canadian scientists have contributed greatly to the world.
181	The Canadian who invented the system of standard time zones was <u>Sir Sandford Fleming</u>. (Reginald Fassenden contributed to the invention of radio. Alexander Graham Bell thought of the telephone at his summer house in Canada. Dr. John A. Hopps invented the pacemaker).
182	The British North America Act of 1867 (known now as the Constitution Act, 1867) defined <u>the responsibilities of the provincial and federal governments of Canada.</u> Each province has a Legislative Assembly which it elects.
183	Canada's type of government is a <u>parliamentary democracy</u>. If the Cabinet ministers receive a "no-confidence" vote, they must resign.
184	The three parts of Parliament are: the Senate, the House of Commons, and <u>the Sovereign</u>. The provinces have legislatures that are comprised of the elected Assembly and the Governor of the province.

FILL-IN QUESTIONS

In the federal government, the _____ selects Cabinet members and is responsible for government policy and operations.	**185**
When a bill is considered read for the first time and is printed, it is at step 1, called the _____.	**186**
Members debate and vote on a bill in the _____.	**187**
The minimum age at which Canadians can vote is ___.	**188**
In Canada the head of state is the Sovereign. The head of government is the _____.	**189**
The three branches of government are the Executive, Legislative and _____.	**190**
Members of the House of Parliament are also called _____.	**191**
The MPs (Members of Parliament) are chosen by the voters in _____.	**192**

FILL-IN ANSWERS

185	**Prime Minister**. The House of Commons is elected by the people every four years. Senators are appointed by the **Prime Minister**. Laws are passed by both chambers and royal assent (granted by the Governor General).
186	**First Reading**. There are 7 steps in a bill becoming law: 1) First Reading, 2) Second Reading, 3) Committee Stage, 4) Report Stage, 5) Third Reading, 6) Senate, 7) Royal Assent.
187	Members debate and vote on a bill in the **Report Stage**. There are 7 steps in a bill becoming law: 1) First Reading, 2) Second Reading, 3) Committee Stage, 4) Report Stage, 5) Third Reading, 6) Senate, 7) Royal Assent.
188	The minimum age at which Canadians can vote is **18**. Canada is a Constitutional Monarchy. Canada's Head of State is the Sovereign The Commonwealth has 52 member states.
189	**Prime Minister**. The Governor General represents the Sovereign. Each of the 10 provinces has a Lieutenant Governor (appointed by the Governor General on the advice of the Prime Minister).
190	The three branches of government are the Executive, Legislative and **Judicial**. The Premier (of each province) is similar to the Prime Minister.
191	Members of the House of Parliament are also called **MPs or Members of Parliament**. Federal elections are held every 4 years (in October) following the most recent general election. The Prime Minister can ask the Governor General to call an election sooner.
192	The MPs (Members of Parliament) are chosen by the voters in **an electoral district**. Canada has 308 electoral districts (also called constituencies or "ridings"). MPs sit in the House of Commons. The minimum age to run in a federal election is 18.

FILL-IN QUESTIONS

Elections Canada, an agency of parliament, produces a list of eligible voters called the _____.	**193**
The party with the most seats in the House of Commons forms the government (after being invited to do so by the Governor General). If that part holds half the seats or more in the House of Commons, the government it forms is called the _____ government.	**194**
The Cabinet is made up of the Prime Minister and _____.	**195**
The House of Commons presently has members of four major political parties: the Liberal Party, the New Democratic Party, the Bloc Quebecois, and the _____.	**196**
On a voting ballot, you mark an _____ to indicate the name of the candidate that you wish to vote for.	**197**
Laws passed by local or municipal governments are called _____.	**198**
Presumption of innocence (everyone is innocent until proven guilty) is the foundation of the Canadian _____ system.	**199**
Canada has 308 electoral districts (also called constituencies or _____).	**200**

FILL-IN ANSWERS

193	Elections Canada, an agency of parliament produces a list called the <u>National Register of Electors</u>. To vote in a federal election, a person must: 1. be a Canadian citizen, 2. be at least 18 (on voting day), 3. be on the National Register of Electors.
194	<u>majority</u>. (If it holds less than half the seats, it is called the minority government.) After a vote of "no confidence," the Prime Minister usually asks the Governor General to call for an election.
195	The Cabinet is made up of the Prime Minister and <u>Cabinet ministers</u>. The Cabinet makes decisions regarding running the country. Decisions may be questioned by Official Opposition (Opposing party with most members) and by parties not in power (known as opposition parties).
196	The House of Commons presently has members of four major political parties: the Liberal Party, the New Democratic Party, the Bloc Quebecois, and the <u>Conservative Party</u>.
197	On a voting ballot, you mark an <u>X</u> to indicate the name of the candidate that you wish to vote for.
198	Laws passed by local or municipal governments are called <u>by-laws.</u> Municipal or local governments have responsibilities in the following areas: policing, firefighting, emergency services, recycling programs, transportation, community affairs and community health and utilities.
199	Presumption of innocence (everyone is innocent until proven guilty) is the foundation of the Canadian <u>judicial</u> system. Courts settle disputes. Police enforce laws. Due process means that all the legal rights of a person must be respected by the government.
200	Canada has 308 electoral districts (also called constituencies or "<u>ridings</u>").

FILL-IN QUESTIONS

The highest court in Canada is the _____.	**201**
The _____ police enforce federal laws and serve as the provincial police in all territories and provinces, except Quebec and Ontario.	**202**
The _____ is a symbol of government, including the courts, the legislatures, the police services, and the armed forces.	**203**
National Flag day is _____.	**204**
The most popular spectator sport in Canada is _____.	**205**
The animal that is on the five cent coin is a _____.	**206**
The National anthem of Canada is _____.	**207**
The highest honour that a Canadian can receive is _____.	**208**

FILL-IN ANSWERS

201	The highest court in Canada is the <u>Supreme Court of Canada.</u> (Provinces have a number of lesser courts.)
202	The <u>Royal Canadian Mounted Police</u> enforce federal laws and serve as the provincial police in all territories and provinces, except Quebec and Ontario.
203	The <u>Crown</u> is a symbol of government, including the courts, the legislatures, the police services, the armed forces.
204	<u>February 15</u>. The Canadian flag was first raised on February 15, 1965). It has a red-white-red pattern. The Maple leaf is a Canadian symbol. The Coat of arms and motto "A Mari Usque Ad Mare" ("from Sea to Sea") are used on currency, public buildings and government documents.
205	The most popular spectator sport in Canada is <u>ice hockey</u>. The second most popular sport is Canadian football. The sport with the most registered players is soccer.
206	The animal that is on the five cent coin is the <u>beaver</u>.
207	The National anthem of Canada is "<u>O Canada</u>." (The "<u>Royal</u> Anthem" is sung whenever the Queen is to be honored.) Citizens who are worthy of recognition are awarded the "Order of Canada."
208	The highest honour that a Canadian can receive is <u>The Victoria Cross (V.C.).</u>

FILL-IN QUESTIONS

Sir John A. Macdonald Day is celebrated on _____.	209
Remembrance Day is celebrated _____.	210
Today more than 75% of Canadians work in _____ industries.	211
The biggest trading partner of Canada is _____.	212
The second largest country in the world is _____.	213
Canada has ___ distinct regions.	214
The national capital of Canada is _____.	215
Canada has ___ provinces.	216

FILL-IN ANSWERS

209	Sir John A. Macdonald Day is celebrated on <u>January 11</u>. Vimy Day – April 9 Victoria Day – Monday preceding May 25 (Sovereign birthday) Fete Nationale (Quebec) June 24 (Feast of St. John the Baptist)
210	Remembrance Day is celebrated <u>NOVEMBER 11</u>. Also remember: Sir Wilfrid Laurier Day – November 20 Christmas – December 25 Boxing Day – December 26
211	Today more than 75% of Canadians work in <u>Service</u> industries.
212	The biggest trading partner of Canada is <u>the U.S.A.</u> The U.S.A. and Canadian border is the world's longest undefended border.
213	The second largest country in the world is <u>Canada</u>. Canada is bordered by the Atlantic Ocean, Pacific Ocean and the U.S.A.
214	Canada has <u>5</u> distinct regions. The 5 regions are: 1. The Atlantic Provinces; 2. The Prairie Provinces; 3. The Northern Territories; 5. Ontario and Quebec; 5. The West Coast
215	The national capital of Canada is <u>Ottawa</u>. (In 1857 Queen Victoria selected Ottawa as the capital.)
216	Canada has <u>10</u> provinces. Canada has 10 provinces and 3 territories. (Memorize the capitals of your province or territory and the capital of Canada.)

FILL-IN QUESTIONS

The population of Canada is ___ million (year 2010).	217
The capital of Nova Scotia is _____.	218
The capital of Ontario is _____.	219
_____ is the oldest colony and the province with the most easterly point in North America, and also known for its fisheries.	220
The only officially bilingual province is _____.	221
The largest city in Canada is Toronto. It is located in the province of _____.	222
The two provinces known as the Prairie Provinces are Manitoba and _____.	223
The Prairie Province that is most populous is _____.	224

FILL-IN ANSWERS

217	The population of Canada is <u>33</u> million. Most Canadians live in cities.
218	The capital of Nova Scotia is <u>Halifax</u>. Also memorize: Newfoundland and Labrador – St. John's New Brunswick – Fredericton Prince Edward Island - Charlottetown
219	<u>Toronto</u>. Also: Quebec – Quebec City; Manitoba – Winnipeg; Saskatchewan – Regina; Alberta – Edmonton; British Columbia – Victoria; Nanavut – Igaluit; Northwest Territories – Yellowknife; Yukon Territory - Whitehorse
220	<u>Newfoundland and Labrador</u> is the oldest colony and the province with the most easterly point in North America, and also known for its fisheries. The smallest province is Prince Edward Island. The Atlantic province with the most population is Nova Scotia.
221	The only officially bilingual province is <u>New Brunswick</u>. Most people in Canada (more than half) live in Ontario and Quebec. In Quebec three-quarters of the people speak French as their first language.
222	The largest city in Canada is Toronto. It is located in the province of <u>Ontario</u>. Ontario has 12 million people and has the Niagara region.
223	The two provinces known as the Prairie Provinces are Manitoba and <u>Saskatchewan</u>. Saskatchewan is known as the "breadbasket of the world" and the "wheat province."
224	The Prairie Province that is most populous is <u>Alberta</u>. The Province was named after Princess Louise Caroline Alberta, the fourth daughter of Queen Victoria.

A/B MULTIPLE CHOICE QUESTIONS

We swear (or affirm) true allegiance to: A. Canada's flag B. Her Majesty Queen Elizabeth the Second, Queen of Canada	**225**
Who personifies Canada? A. every citizen B. our Sovereign	**226**
Immigrants and settlers have been coming to Canada for: A. 400 years B. 500 years	**227**
Which of the following choices is correct? Canada is: A. a parliamentary democracy B. a dictatorship	**228**

A/B MULTIPLE CHOICE ANSWERS

225	B. Her Majesty Queen Elizabeth the Second, Queen of Canada We swear (or affirm) true allegiance to Her Majesty Queen Elizabeth the Second, Queen of Canada.
226	B. our Sovereign, Queen Elizabeth the Second Our Sovereign, Queen Elizabeth the Second, personifies Canada.
227	A. 400 years Immigrants and settlers have been coming to Canada for 400 years.
228	A. a parliamentary democracy Canada is a parliamentary democracy.

A/B MULTIPLE CHOICE QUESTIONS

To become a Canadian citizen, a person between the ages of _____ must have adequate knowledge of French or English.

A. 18 and 54
B. 16 and 55

229

Which of the following choices is NOT correct? To become a Canadian citizen, a person must learn about:

A. U.S. history
B. Canada's history

230

How old does an applicant have to be NOT to be required to write the citizenship test?

A. 45
B. 55

231

A Notice to Appear to Take the Oath of Citizenship is given to a citizenship applicant:

A. as soon as the application is filed.
B. after the applicant passes the test.

232

A/B MULTIPLE CHOICE ANSWERS

229	**A. 18 and 54** **To become a Canadian citizen, a person between the ages of 18 and 54 must have adequate knowledge of French or English.**
230	**A. U.S. history** **To become a Canadian citizen, a person must learn about <u>Canada's</u> history.**
231	**B. 55** **For an applicant not to be required to write the citizenship test, the applicant must be at least 55 years old (or under 18).**
232	**B. after the applicant passes the test.** **A Notice to Appear to Take the Oath of Citizenship is given to a citizenship applicant after the applicant passes the test.**

A/B MULTIPLE CHOICE QUESTIONS

At the Oath of Citizenship Ceremony, the applicant:

A. must write the test.
B. takes the Oath of Citizenship.

233

If an applicant does not pass the Citizenship Test, the applicant:

A. cannot take the test ever again.
B. receives a notification indicating the next steps.

234

What is the significance of wearing a red poppy?

A. It looks pretty.
B. We wear it to remember Canadians who died in war.

235

At the ceremony, an applicant for citizenship:

A. takes the Oath of Citizenship.
B. must pay a citizenship fee.

236

A/B MULTIPLE CHOICE ANSWERS

233	**B. takes the Oath of Citizenship.** At the Oath of Citizenship Ceremony, the applicant takes the Oath of Citizenship.
234	**B. receives a notification indicating the next steps.** If an applicant does not pass the Citizenship Test, the applicant receives a notification indicating the next steps.
235	**B. We wear it to remember Canadians who died in war.**
236	**A. takes the Oath of Citizenship.** At the ceremony, an applicant for citizenship takes the Oath of Citizenship.

A/B MULTIPLE CHOICE QUESTIONS

Which of the following is a source of Canadian law? A. the civil code of France B. laws enacted by the North Atlantic Treaty Organization	237
The Magna Carta, signed in 1215, is also known as : A. the Constitution B. the Great Charter of Freedoms	238
The Magna Carta ensures: A. freedom from jail and paying taxes. B. freedom of conscience and religion.	239
Which of the following 2 rights are included in the Magna Carta? A. Freedom of thought, belief, opinion and expression, including freedom of speech and of the press B. Freedom of peaceful assembly C. Both A and B.	240

A/B MULTIPLE CHOICE ANSWERS

237	A. the Civil Code of France. Sources of Canadian law are: 1. the civil code of France 2. English common law and laws passed by the provincial legislatures and parliament 3. Great Britain's unwritten constitution
238	B. the Great Charter of Freedoms The Magna Carta, signed in 1215, is also known as the Great Charter of Freedoms.
239	B. freedom of conscience and religion The Magna Carta ensures freedom of conscience and religion.
240	C. Both A and B. The Magna Carta includes the following freedoms: Freedom of conscience and religion; Freedom of thought, belief, opinion and expression, including freedom of speech and of the press; Freedom of peaceful assembly; Freedom of association.

A/B MULTIPLE CHOICE QUESTIONS

A legal procedure designed to challenge the unlawful detention of a person by the state is known as:

A. detention.
B. habeas corpus.

241

In 1982 the Canadian Constitution was amended to include the:

A. Canadian Charter of Rights and Freedoms.
B. Magna Carta.

242

The words "Whereas Canada is founded upon principles that recognize the supremacy of God and the rule of law-" are the first words in:

A. the Constitution of Canada.
B. the Magna Carta.

243

The Canadian Charter of Rights and Freedoms was entrenched in the Constitution of Canada in the year _____.

A. 1812
B. 1982

244

A/B MULTIPLE CHOICE ANSWERS

241	**B. habeas corpus** A legal procedure designed to challenge the unlawful detention of a person by the state is known as habeas corpus.
242	**A. Canadian Charter of Rights and Freedoms.** In 1982 the Canadian Constitution was amended to include the Canadian Charter of Rights and Freedoms.
243	**A. the Constitution of Canada.** The words "Whereas Canada is founded upon principles that recognize the supremacy of God and the rule of law-" are the first words in the Constitution of Canada.
244	**B. 1982** It begins with the words, "Whereas Canada is founded upon principles that recognize the supremacy of God and the rule of law."

A/B MULTIPLE CHOICE QUESTIONS

The Canadian Charter of Rights and Freedoms summarizes fundamental freedoms, including Official Language Rights and Minority Language Educational Rights. Under this charter:

A. all languages are official languages
B. Both French and English are official languages.

245

Men and women in Canada:

A. have different rights under the law.
B. are equal under the law.

246

Which of the following is NOT a citizenship responsibility?

A. obeying the law
B. participating in sports

247

In Canada:

A. military service is not compulsory.
B. you must serve in the army.

248

A/B MULTIPLE CHOICE ANSWERS

245	**B. Both French and English are official languages.** **The charter also sets out other rights relating to: Mobility rights, Aboriginal People's' Rights, and Multiculturalism.**
246	**B. are equal under the law.** **Persons who are guilty of crimes such as "honour killings" and other similar criminal acts are punished by Canadian law.**
247	**B. participating in sports** **Other citizenship responsibilities include serving on a jury, voting in elections, taking responsibility for oneself and one's family, helping others in the community and protecting and enjoying our heritage and environment.**
248	**A. military service is <u>not</u> compulsory.** **Serving in the Canadian Forces or helping in the community is voluntary.**

A/B MULTIPLE CHOICE QUESTIONS

Canadian Aboriginal peoples migrated from Asia: A. in the 1800's. B. many thousands of years ago.	249
The three groups referred to with the term Aboriginal Peoples are: A. Comanche, Aztec and Huron. B. Indian (First Nations), Inuit and Métis.	250
Who said that immigrant groups, "should retain their individuality and each make its contribution to the national character" and that immigrant groups could learn "from the other, and ... while they cherish their own special loyalties and traditions, they cherish not less that new loyalty and tradition which springs from their union." A. John Buchan, 1st Baron Tweedsmuir and Governor General of Canada from 1935 – 1940. B. King Henry III	251
Some Nations people live in about 600 communities: A. on reserve land. B. in Toronto	252

A/B MULTIPLE CHOICE ANSWERS

249	**B. many thousands of years ago** **The Canadian Constitution contains aboriginal and treaty rights. (King George III in the Royal Proclamation of 1763 stated the basis for negotiating treaties between the aboriginals and newcomers.)**
250	**B. Indian (First Nations), Inuit and Métis.** **(From about 1800 – 1980, children of aboriginal peoples were forced to be educated in residential schools.)**
251	**A. John Buchan, 1st Baron Tweedsmuir and Governor General of Canada from 1935 – 1940.**
252	**A. on reserve land.** **Others live off-reserve (usually in urban areas).**

A/B MULTIPLE CHOICE QUESTIONS

The name of this group means "the people." They speak the Inuktitut language and live in the arctic region.

A. Métis
B. Inuit

253

The people that have both Aboriginal and European ancestry are called:

A. Inuit
B. Métis

254

Which of the following percentages relating to Aboriginal people are correct?

A. First Nations (65%), Métis (30%), Inuit (4%)
B. First Nations (33%), Métis (33%), Inuit (33)

255

The two official languages of Canada are:

A. English and Spanish
B. English and French

256

A/B MULTIPLE CHOICE ANSWERS

253	**B. Inuit** The arctic is harsh. To live there, the Inuit have gathered great knowledge about the wildlife and land of the arctic.
254	**B. Métis** The Métis have both English and French speaking backgrounds. They also speak their own Michif dialect.
255	**A. First Nations (65%), Métis (30%), Inuit (4%)** Aboriginal peoples are those whose ancestors migrated to Canada from Asia thousands of years ago.
256	**B. English and French** (18 million English speaking "Anglophones" and 7 million French speaking "Francophones.") Most French speaking people reside in the province of Quebec. One province (New Brunswick) is the only province that is officially bilingual.

A/B MULTIPLE CHOICE QUESTIONS

Since 1604 French colonists settled in the Maritime provinces. The descendants of these settlers are called _____.

A. aboriginal
B. Acadians

257

People of Quebec are called Quebecers. Most speak French, but about one million Anglo-Quebecers speak ____.

A. English
B. Spanish

258

Many recent immigrants to Canada (since 1970) come from _____.

A. Europe
B. Asia

259

In two of the biggest cities of Canada, English is the most popular spoken language at home, followed by _____.

A. Italian
B. Chinese

260

A/B MULTIPLE CHOICE ANSWERS

257	**B. Acadians** Two thirds of Acadians were deported from their area between 1755 and 1763 (during the "Great Upheaval" – during the Britain/French war).
258	**A. English** Anglo-Quebecers are descendants of Irish, Welsh, Scottish and English settlers. They are called English Canadians.
259	**B. Asia** Because of Canada's immigration, Canada is also spoken of as being the "land of immigrants." The most numerous people living in Canada are: English, French, Scottish, Irish, German, Italian, Chinese, Aboriginal, Ukranian, Dutch, South Asian, and Scandinavian.
260	**B. Chinese** Also, the majority of Canadians identify with Christianity.

A/B MULTIPLE CHOICE QUESTIONS

The first Europeans exploring Canada called the native people _____ because they believed that they were in the East Indies.

A. Europeans
B. Indians

261

After Aboriginals came into contact with Europeans, many died of diseases to which they lacked _____.

A. contact
B. immunity

262

What is the name of the people that colonized Greenland (1,000 years ago) and also visited Newfoundland and Labrador?

A. English
B. Vikings

263

The name Canada comes from an Iroquoian (Indian tribe) word "kanata," which means:

A. country
B. village

264

A/B MULTIPLE CHOICE ANSWERS

261	**B. Indians** Some Indians were hunters, farmers, nomadic and some were hunter-gatherers.
262	**B. immunity** In spite of this, in the first 200 years of Canada's history, there existed military and economic bonds between the Aboriginals and the settlers.
263	**B. Vikings** (In 1497 John Cabot (Italian immigrant to England) drew a map of Canada's east coast. Jacques Cartier (French) between 1534 and 1542 claimed the land for the King of France, King Francis I).
264	**B. village** The name Canada comes from an Iroquoian (Indian tribe) word "kanata," which means <u>village</u>. The name "Canada" first appeared on maps.

A/B MULTIPLE CHOICE QUESTIONS

In 1604 European settlements were established by French explorers Pierre de Monts and:

A. Vasco de Gama
B. Samuel de Champlain

265

Samuel de Champlain made an alliance with:

A. the Iroquois
B. Huron, Montagnais and Algonquin

266

The company that King Charles II (1670) granted exclusive trading rights in Hudson Bay area was called:

A. Hudson's Bay Company
B. Fur Traders, Inc.

267

The British defeated the French in the year _____ in the Battle of the Plains of Abraham at Quebec City. This ended the French Empire in America.

A. 1600
B. 1759

268

A/B MULTIPLE CHOICE ANSWERS

265	**B. Samuel de Champlain** The settlements were established on St. Croix Island and Port-Royal. (St. Croix Island is in Maine (US) and at Port-Royal in Acadia (Canada)).
266	**B. Huron, Montagnais and Algonquin** The Iroquois and the French battled for almost a century. They made peace in the year 1701. (The Iroquois were enemies with the Huron, Montagnais and Algonquin.) The Aboriginal peoples and the French established a fur-trade economy. Under the leadership of leaders such as Count Frontenac, Jean Talon and Bishop Laval, the French Empire spread from the Atlantic coast (Hudson Bay) to the Gulf of Mexico.
267	**A. Hudson's Bay Company** Furs were often collected by traders who often travelled by canoe. They formed contracts with the First Nations. These traders are referred to as "coureurs des bois" and "voyageurs".
268	**B. 1759** Brigadier James Wolfe led the British soldiers and the Marquis de Montcalm led the French soldiers. They were both killed in the battle.

A/B MULTIPLE CHOICE QUESTIONS

The people living in the "Province of Quebec" under the English speaking British Empire are known as:

A. English
B. habitants or Canadiens

269

Around 1776 some people loyal to the King fled the American colonies and settled in Nova Scotia and Quebec. These people were called _____.

A. settlers
B. Loyalists

270

Which Act in 1791 divided the Province of Quebec into Upper Canada (present day Ontario) and Lower Canada (present day Quebec)?

A. The Constitutional Act of 1791.
B. The Freedom Act of 1791.

271

Slavery was abolished in the province of Upper Canada in 1793. Its first Lieutenant Governor was Lieutenant Colonel John Graves Simcoe. He founded the City of York whose present day name is _____.

A. Quebec City
B. Toronto

272

A/B MULTIPLE CHOICE ANSWERS

269	**B. habitants or Canadiens** In 1774, the British Parliament passed the "Quebec Act of 1774." This act permitted French speaking Catholic people to hold public office. This act also established French civil law and English criminal law.
270	**B. Loyalists** Some of these black Loyalists (freed slaves) settled in Nova Scotia. In 1792 some moved to Africa and established Freetown in Sierra Leone (West Africa).
271	**A. The Constitutional Act of 1791.** Upper Canada was mainly English speaking and Lower Canada was mainly French speaking. "British North America" generally referred to as the two Canadas (Upper and Lower) and the Atlantic colonies.
272	**B. Toronto** In 1807 the buying and selling of slaves was abolished by the British Parliament. In 1833 it was abolished throughout the empire.

A/B MULTIPLE CHOICE QUESTIONS

Mary Ann (Shadd) Carey was the first woman publisher in Canada. In 1853 she founded and edited the Provincial Freeman, which encouraged:

A. separation from British rule.
B. anti-slavery and black immigration to Canada.

273

In the 1800's Canadian financial institutions began to emerge. In 1832 the _____ Stock exchange opened.

A. Johnston
B. Montreal

274

The USA invaded Canada in the year _____.

A. 1776
B. 1812

275

The rebellion of 1837-38 happened mainly because some people thought that:

A. Canada should be divided.
B. democracy was not coming fast enough to Canada.

276

A/B MULTIPLE CHOICE ANSWERS

273	**B. anti-slavery and black immigration to Canada.** She also supported British rule and drinking less alcohol.
274	**B. Montreal** Before the 1800's the economy of Canada relied mainly on its natural resources (fish, timber, furs, etc.) and on farming.
275	**B. 1812** In 1813 the Americans burned government buildings in Toronto. The border between the U.S. and Canada is one of the results of the War of 1812.
276	**B. democracy was not coming fast enough to Canada.** Also, some Canadians were in favor of joining the United States.

A/B MULTIPLE CHOICE QUESTIONS

The person who suggested that Lower Canada and Upper Canada be merged and given "responsible government" was: A. Lord Durham B. John Cabot	277
The Province of Canada was the result of the 1840 unification of: A. Quebec and Montreal B. Upper and Lower Canada	278
The "Dominion of Canada" was established by the Fathers of Confederation in 1867. Which of the following are Fathers of Confederation? A. Lord Durham, John Cabot, Major General Robert Ross B. Sir Étienne-Paschal Taché, Sir George-Étienne Cartier, Sir John A. McDonald	279
On July 1, 1867 the Fathers of Confederation established Canada. July 1 was celebrated as "Dominion Day" until 1982. However, today "Dominion Day" is called: A. Unity Day B. Canada Day	280

A/B MULTIPLE CHOICE ANSWERS

277	**A. Lord Durham** "Responsible government," recommended by Lord Durham, meant that the ministers of the Crown to govern needed first the support of the majority of the elected representatives of the Canadian people. (He mistakenly suggested that all Canadiens needed to be assimilated into the culture of the English Protestants.)
278	**B. Upper and Lower Canada** "Responsible government" in the Province of Canada was advanced by reformers such as Robert Baldwin, Sir Louis-Hippolyte La Fontaine and Joseph Howe. In 1848-49 responsible government was introduced in Canada by Lord Elgin, governor of United Canada.
279	**B. Sir Etienne-Paschal Tache, Sir George-Étienne Cartier, Sir John A. McDonald** Two levels of government (federal and provincial) were introduced.
280	**B. Canada Day** The term "Dominion of Canada" was suggested by Sir Leonard Tilley, one of the Fathers of Confederation, in the year 1864.

A/B MULTIPLE CHOICE QUESTIONS

Which of the following groups became part of Canada first?

A. Ontario, Quebec, Nova Scotia, New Brunswick
B. Manitoba, Northwest Territories (N.W.T.)

281

Canada's first Prime Minister (1867) was:

A. Sir George-Étienne Cartier
B. Sir John Alexander Macdonald

282

This Canadien was from Quebec and a key architect of Confederation.

A. Sir George-Étienne Cartier
B. Sir Sam Steele

283

Prime Minister Macdonald in 1873 established:

A. the NWMP (North West Mounted Police).
B. Fort Garry

284

A/B MULTIPLE CHOICE ANSWERS

281	**A. Ontario, Quebec, Nova Scotia, New Brunswick (in 1867)** **(1870) Manitoba, Northwest Territories (N.W.T.)** **(1871) British Columbia** **(1873) Prince Edward Island** **(1880) Transfer of Arctic Islands to N.W.T** **(1898) Yukon Territory** **(1905) Saskatchewan, Alberta** **(1949) Newfoundland and Labrador; (1999) Nanavut**
282	**B. Sir John Alexander Macdonald** **Sir John Alexander Macdonald's portrait is on the $10 bill.** **On January 11 we celebrate Sir John A. Macdonald Day.**
283	**A. Sir George-Étienne Cartier** **Sir George-Étienne Cartier also was instrumental in the negotiations for the following territories to enter into Canada: Manitoba, Northwest Territories, and British Columbia.**
284	**A. the NWMP (North West Mounted Police).** **The NWMP (now RCMP: Royal Canadian Mounted Police) are Canada's national police force.** **The NWMP were established after the first Métis uprising.** **Two great Métis leaders were Louis Riel (father of Manitoba) and Gabriel Dumont.**

A/B MULTIPLE CHOICE QUESTIONS

The first French-Canadian prime minister since confederation, Sir Wilfrid Laurier, is on which the following bills?

A. $1 bill
B. $5 bill

285

The person known as "Canada's greatest soldier" is:

A. Sir Arthur Currie
B. Emily Stowe

286

The founder of the woman's suffrage movement in Canada was:

A. Emile Bronte
B. Dr. Emily Stowe

287

Remembrance Day is observed on:

A. January 21
B. November 11

288

A/B MULTIPLE CHOICE ANSWERS

285	**B. $5 bill** Sir Wilfrid Laurier encouraged people to immigrate to the West. Immigration was helped by the railway from Sea to Sea, completed in 1885. It was built mostly by European and Chinese labour.
286	**A. Sir Arthur Currie** Sir Arthur Currie fought in WWI. Canadian troops also fought in the South African War (1899-1902).
287	**B. Dr. Emily Stowe** Nurses were granted the right to vote in 1917 and most Canadian female citizens over 21 in 1918.
288	**B. November 11** On Remembrance Day we remember the sacrifice of 110,000 Canadians who gave their lives in wars. We wear the <u>red poppy</u> and observe a moment of silence. The poem "In Flanders Fields" was composed by Lt. Col. John McCrae. It was composed in 1915 and is recited on Remembrance Day.

A/B MULTIPLE CHOICE QUESTIONS

The British Commonwealth of Nations is a free association of states. It evolved:

A. in the 1700's.
B. after the First Word War.

289

In this battle of WWII, one in ten of the Allied soldiers was Canadian.

A. Battle of Hastings
B. D-Day

290

The Act which guarantees health insurance coverage to Canadians is:

A. The Suffrage Act
B. The Canada Health Act

291

Which Act guarantees French language rights and services in all of Canada?

A. The Suffrage Act
B. The Official Languages Act

292

A/B MULTIPLE CHOICE ANSWERS

289	**B. after the First Word War.** **The Commonwealth includes Canada, Australia, India, some African countries and some Caribbean countries.**
290	**B. D-Day** **In the second World War (1939-1945), more than one million Canadians served in the armed forces.**
291	**B. The Canada Health Act** **Unemployment insurance was introduced in 1940 by the Canadian government.** **Education is provided by the provinces and territories.**
292	**B. The Official Languages Act**

A/B MULTIPLE CHOICE QUESTIONS

The "Group of Seven" (founded in 1920) developed:

A. a style of painting
B. military maneuvers

293

The sport of basketball was invented by:

A. Donovan Bailey in 1886.
B. James Naismith in 1891

294

The Canadian who invented the worldwide system of standard time zones was:

A. Alexander Graham Bell
B. Sir Sandford Fleming

295

The British North America Act of 1867 (now known as the Constitution Act, 1867):

A. extended health care to all Canadians.
B. defined the responsibilities of the provincial and federal governments of Canada.

296

A/B MULTIPLE CHOICE ANSWERS

293	**A. a style of painting** **The "Group of Seven" (founded in 1920) developed a style of painting.**
294	**B. James Naismith in 1891** **Sports in Canada are popular in all provinces.** **Canadian scientists have contributed greatly to the world.**
295	**B. Sir Sandford Fleming** **(Reginald Fassenden contributed to the invention of the radio.** **Dr. John A. Hopps invented the pacemaker)**
296	**B. defined the responsibilities of the provincial and federal governments of Canada.** **Each province has an elected Legislative Assembly.**

A/B MULTIPLE CHOICE QUESTIONS

Canada's type of government is: A. republican monarchy B. a parliamentary democracy	297
The three parts of Parliament are: the Sovereign, the Senate, and: A. House of Commons B. Constitutional Convention	298
In the federal government, who selects Cabinet members and is responsible for government policy and operations? A. the Senators B. the Prime Minister	299
When a bill is considered read for the first time and is printed, it is at step 1, called the: A. First Reading B. Second Reading	300

A/B MULTIPLE CHOICE ANSWERS

297	**B. a parliamentary democracy** If the Cabinet ministers receive a "no-confidence" vote, they must resign.
298	**A. House of Commons** The provinces have legislatures that are comprised of the elected Assembly and the Governor of the province.
299	**B. the Prime Minister** The House of Commons is elected by the people every four years. Senators are appointed by the Prime Minister. Laws are passed by both chambers and royal assent (granted by the Governor General).
300	**A. First Reading** There are 7 steps in a bill becoming law: 1) First Reading, 2) Second Reading, 3) Committee Stage, 4) Report Stage, 5) Third Reading, 6) Senate, 7) Royal Assent.

A/B MULTIPLE CHOICE QUESTIONS

In this step, Members debate and vote on a bill:

A. First Reading
B. Report Stage

301

The minimum age at which Canadians can vote is:

A. 14
B. 18

302

In Canada the head of state is the Sovereign. The head of government is:

A. the Assembly
B. the Prime Minister

303

The three branches of government are the Executive, Legislative and:

A. the people
B. Judicial

304

A/B MULTIPLE CHOICE ANSWERS

301	**B. Report Stage** There are 7 steps in a bill becoming law: 1) First Reading, 2) Second Reading, 3) Committee Stage, 4) Report Stage, 5) Third Reading, 6) Senate, 7) Royal Assent.
302	**B. 18** Canada is a Constitutional Monarchy. Canada's Head of State is the Sovereign. The Commonwealth has 52 member states.
303	**B. the Prime Minister** The Governor General represents the Sovereign. Each of the 10 provinces has a Lieutenant Governor (appointed by the Governor General on the advice of the Prime Minister).
304	**B. Judicial** The Premier (of each province) is similar to the Prime Minister.

A/B MULTIPLE CHOICE QUESTIONS

Members of the House of Parliament are also called:

A. MPs or Members of Parliament
B. Dukes

305

The MP (Member of Parliament) is chosen by the voters in:

A. a province
B. an electoral district

306

Elections Canada, is an agency of parliament which produces a list called:

A. National Register of Electors
B. National List

307

The party with the most seats in the House of Commons forms the government (after being invited to do so by the Governor General). If that party holds half or more of the seats in the House of Commons, the government is called:

A. the minority government
B. the majority government

308

A/B MULTIPLE CHOICE ANSWERS

305	**A. MPs or Members of Parliament** Federal elections are held every 4 years (in October) following the most recent general election. The prime Minister can ask the Governor General to call an election sooner.
306	**B. an electoral district** Canada has 308 electoral districts (also called constituencies or "ridings"). MPs sit in the House of Commons. The minimum age to run in a federal election is 18.
307	**A. National Register of Electors** To vote in a federal election, a person must: 1. be a Canadian citizen, 2. be at least 18 (on voting day), and 3. be on the National Register of Electors.
308	**B. the majority government** (If it holds less than half the seats, it is called the minority government.) After a vote of "no confidence" the Prime Minister usually asks the Governor General to call for an election.

A/B MULTIPLE CHOICE QUESTIONS

The Cabinet is made up of the Prime Minister and the _____. A. Assemblymen B. Cabinet ministers	309
The House of Commons presently has members of four major political parties: the Liberal Party, the New Democratic Party, the Bloc Quebecois, and: A. the Conservative Party. B. Populist Party.	310
On a voting ballot, what do you mark to indicate the name of the candidate of your choice? A. AOK B. X	311
Canada is bordered by the U.S.A, the Atlantic Ocean, and _____. A. the Gulf of Mexico B. the Pacific Ocean	312

A/B MULTIPLE CHOICE ANSWERS

309	**B. Cabinet ministers** The Cabinet makes decisions regarding how the country is run. These decisions may be questioned by the Official Opposition (Opposing party with the most members) and by parties not in power (known as opposition parties).
310	**A. the Conservative Party.** The House of Commons now has members of four major political parties: the Liberal Party, the New Democratic Party, the Bloc Quebecois, and the <u>Conservative Party</u>.
311	**B. X** Election results are made public on television and on the Elections Canada website (www.elections.ca).
312	**B. the Pacific Ocean**

A/B MULTIPLE CHOICE QUESTIONS

Laws passed by local or municipal governments are called:

A. by-laws
B. major laws

313

Presumption of innocence (everyone is innocent until proven guilty) is the foundation of:

A. our judicial system
B. our political system

314

The highest court in Canada is:

A. Provincial Court
B. Supreme Court of Canada

315

The following police enforce federal laws and serve as the provincial police in all territories and provinces, except Quebec and Ontario:

A. the city police
B. the Royal Canadian Mounted Police

316

A/B MULTIPLE CHOICE ANSWERS

313	**A. by-laws** **Municipal or local governments have responsibilities in: policing, firefighting, emergency services, recycling programs, transportation, community affairs and community health and utilities.**
314	**A. our judicial system** **Courts settle disputes. Police enforce laws.** **Due process means that the legal rights of a person must be respected by the government.**
315	**B. Supreme Court of Canada** **(Provinces have a number of lesser courts.)**
316	**B. the Royal Canadian Mounted Police (RCMP)**

A/B MULTIPLE CHOICE QUESTIONS

Which of the following is a symbol of government, courts, the legislatures, the police services, and the armed forces?

A. the parliament building
B. the Crown

317

National Flag day is:

A. February 15
B. March 15

318

The most popular spectator sport in Canada is:

A. baseball
B. ice hockey

319

The animal that is on the five cent coin is the:

A. beaver
B. eagle

320

A/B MULTIPLE CHOICE ANSWERS

317	**B. the Crown**
318	**A. February 15** **National Flag day is February 15 (the Canadian flag was first raised on February 15, 1965). It has a red-white-red pattern.** **The Maple leaf is also a Canadian symbol.** **The coat of arms and the motto "A Mari Usque Ad Mare" which means "from Sea to Sea" are used on currency, public buildings and government documents.**
319	**B. ice hockey** **The second most popular sport is Canadian football.** **The sport with the most registered players is soccer.**
320	**A. beaver** **The animal that is on the five cent coin is the beaver.**

A/B MULTIPLE CHOICE QUESTIONS

The National anthem of Canada is:

A. Our Country
B. O Canada

321

The highest honour that a Canadian can receive is:

A. The Victoria Cross (V.C.)
B. The Medal of Honour

322

Which of the following holiday dates is NOT correct?

A. New Year's day – January 1
B. Sir John A. Macdonald Day – February 11

323

Which of the following holiday date is NOT correct?

A. Canada Day – July 1
B. Remembrance Day – November 15

324

A/B MULTIPLE CHOICE ANSWERS

321	**B. O Canada** (The "Royal Anthem" is sung when the Queen is to be honored.) Citizens who are worthy of recognition are awarded the "Order of Canada."
322	**A. The Victoria Cross (V.C.)** The highest honour that a Canadian can receive is The Victoria Cross (V.C.).
323	**B. Sir John A. Macdonald Day – February 11** (Sir John A. McDonald Day is celebrated JANUARY 11.) Also remember: Vimy Day – April 9 Victoria Day – Monday preceding May 25 (Sovereign birthday) Fete Nationale (Quebec) June 24 (Feast of St. John the Baptist)
324	**B. Remembrance Day – November 15** Remembrance Day is celebrated NOVEMBER 11. Also remember: Sir Wilfrid Laurier Day – November 20 Christmas – December 25 Boxing Day – December 26

A/B MULTIPLE CHOICE QUESTIONS

Today more than 75% of Canadians work in:

A. Manufacturing industries
B. Service industries

325

The biggest trading partner of Canada is:

A. Mexico
B. U.S.A.

326

The second largest country in the world is:

A. China
B. Canada

327

Canada has ___ distinct regions.

A. 3
B. 5

328

A/B MULTIPLE CHOICE ANSWERS

325	**B. Service industries**
326	**B. U.S.A.** **The U.S.A. and Canadian border is the world's longest undefended border.**
327	**B. Canada** **Canada is bordered by the Atlantic Ocean, Pacific Ocean and the U.S.A.**
328	**B. 5 The 5 regions are:** **1. The Atlantic Provinces** **2. The Prairie Provinces** **3. The Northern Territories** **4. Ontario and Quebec** **5. The West Coast**

A/B MULTIPLE CHOICE QUESTIONS

The national capital of Canada is: A. Montreal B. Ottawa	329
Canada has ____ provinces. A. 8 B. 10	330
The population of Canada in 2010 is: A. 20 million B. 33 million	331
Which of the following is NOT the correct capital for the province or territory listed? A. Newfoundland and Labrador – St. John's B. Prince Edward Island - Albany	332

A/B MULTIPLE CHOICE ANSWERS

329	**B. Ottawa** **(In 1857 Queen Victoria chose Ottawa as the capital.)**
330	**B. 10** **Canada has 10 provinces and 3 territories.** **(Memorize the capitals of your province or territory and the capital of Canada.)**
331	**B. 33 million** **Most Canadians live in cities.**
332	**B. Prince Edward Island – Albany** **(The capital of Prince Edward Island is <u>Charlottetown</u>.)**

A/B MULTIPLE CHOICE QUESTIONS

Which of the following is NOT the correct capital for the province or territory listed? A. Quebec – Quebec City B. Saskatchewan – King	333
The oldest colony is the province with the most easterly point in North America, and is also known for its fisheries: A. Prince Edward Island B. Newfoundland and Labrador	334
The only officially bilingual province is: A. New Brunswick B. Ontario	335
The largest city in Canada is Toronto. It is located in the province of: A. Quebec B. Ontario	336

A/B MULTIPLE CHOICE ANSWERS

333	**B. Saskatchewan – King** **The capital of Saskatchewan is <u>Regina</u>.** **Also:** **Alberta – Edmonton** **British Columbia – Victoria** **Nanavut – Igaluit** **Northwest Territories – Yellowknife** **Yukon Territory - Whitehorse**
334	**B. Newfoundland and Labrador** **The smallest province is Prince Edward Island.** **The Atlantic province with the most population is Nova Scotia.**
335	**A. New Brunswick** **Most people in Canada (more than half) live in Ontario and Quebec. In Quebec three-quarters of the people speak French as their first language.**
336	**B. Ontario** **Ontario has 12 million people and has the Niagara region.**

A/B MULTIPLE CHOICE QUESTIONS

The two provinces known as the Prairie Provinces are:

A. Manitoba and Saskatchewan
B. Quebec and Ontario

337

The Prairie Province that is most populous is:

A. British Columbia
B. Alberta

338

The Port of Vancouver is found in the Province of:

A. Alberta
B. British Columbia

339

Nanavut and Yukon (Northwest Territories) contain a population of 100,000, but comprise ___ of Canada's land.

A. 1/5
B. 1/3

340

A/B MULTIPLE CHOICE ANSWERS

337	**A. Manitoba and Saskatchewan** Saskatchewan is known as the "breadbasket of the world" and the "wheat province."
338	**B. Alberta** The Province was named after Princess Louise Caroline Alberta, the fourth daughter of Queen Victoria.
339	**B. British Columbia** Chinese and Punjabi are spoken often in the cities, next to English.
340	**B. 1/3** During the 1890's gold rush, thousands of minors came to the Yukon in search of treasure.

A/B/C/D MULTIPLE CHOICE QUESTIONS

We swear (or affirm) true allegiance to:

A. the constitution
B. the flag
C. Canada
D. Her Majesty Queen Elizabeth the Second, Queen of Canada

341

Who personifies Canada?

A. every citizen
B. The Prime Minister
C. Minister of Public Works
D. our Sovereign, Queen Elizabeth the Second

342

Immigrants and settlers have been coming to Canada for:

A. 200 years
B. 300 years
C. 400 years
D. 500 years

343

Which of the following is <u>NOT</u> correct?
A. Responsibilities of citizenship include serving on a jury, obeying the law and taking responsibility for oneself and family.
B. Members of Parliament are elected by the voters in their local constituency (called the "riding")
C. Remembrance Day Poppy reminds us of Canadians who died in war.
D. English and Chinese are the two official languages.

344

A/B/C/D MULTIPLE CHOICE ANSWERS

341	**D. Her Majesty Queen Elizabeth the Second, Queen of Canada**
342	**D. our Sovereign, Queen Elizabeth the Second**
343	**C. 400 years**
344	**D. (Chinese is <u>NOT</u> an official language of Canada)**

A/B/C/D MULTIPLE CHOICE QUESTIONS

Which of the following choices is NOT correct? Canada is:

A. a federal state
B. a parliamentary democracy
C. a dictatorship
C. a constitutional monarchy

345

To become a Canadian citizen, a person between the ages of _____ must have adequate knowledge of French or English.

A. 21 and 62
B. 18 and 54
C. 16 and 55
D. 21 and 54

346

Which of the following choices is NOT correct? To become a Canadian citizen, a person must learn about:

A. U.S. history
B. geography of Canada
C. Canada's history
D. responsibilities of Canadian citizenship

347

How old does an applicant have to be to not be required to write the citizenship test?

A. 18
B. 21
C. 55
D. 34

348

A/B/C/D MULTIPLE CHOICE ANSWERS

345	C. a dictatorship
346	B. 18 and 54
347	A. U.S. history
348	C. 55 (or less than 18)

A/B/C/D MULTIPLE CHOICE QUESTIONS

A Notice to Appear to Take the Oath of Citizenship is given to a citizenship applicant:

A. as soon as the application is filed.
B. before the applicant writes the test.
C. 120 days after applying for citizenship.
D. after the applicant passes the test.

349

At the Oath of Citizenship Ceremony, the applicant:

A. must write the test.
B. must answer 20 questions.
C. receives a Canadian passport.
D. takes the Oath of Citizenship.

350

If an applicant does not pass the Citizenship Test, the applicant:

A. must pay a penalty fee.
B. cannot take the test ever again.
C. must sign the oath form.
D. receives a notification indicating the next steps.

351

Which of the following is false?

At the ceremony, an applicant for citizenship:
A. takes the Oath of Citizenship.
B. signs a form called the "oath form".
C. is given the Canadian Citizenship Certificate.
D. must pay a citizenship fee.

352

A/B/C/D MULTIPLE CHOICE ANSWERS

349	D. after the applicant passes the test.
350	D. takes the Oath of Citizenship.
351	D. receives a notification indicating the next steps.
352	D. must pay a citizenship fee.

A/B/C/D MULTIPLE CHOICE QUESTIONS

Which of the following is <u>NOT</u> a source of Canadian law?

A. the civil code of France
B. English common law and laws passed by the provincial legislatures and parliament.
C. Great Britain's unwritten constitution
D. laws enacted by the North Atlantic Treaty Organization.

353

The Magna Carta, signed in 1215, is also known as:

A. the Constitution
B. the amendment
C. the Great Charter of Freedoms
D. the First Law

354

The Magna Carta ensures:

A. freedom from jail and paying taxes.
B. unfair factory labor
C. freedom from taxes only.
D. freedom of conscience and religion.

355

Which of the following rights are included in the Magna Carta?
   1. Freedom of Association
   2. Freedom of conscience and religion.
A. none of them
B. both freedoms are included in the Magna Carta.
C. Only 1. Freedom of Association
D. Only 2. Freedom of conscience and religion

356

A/B/C/D MULTIPLE CHOICE ANSWERS

353	D. laws enacted by the North Atlantic Treaty Organization.
354	C. the Great Charter of Freedoms
355	D. freedom of conscience and religion
356	B. both freedoms are included in the Magna Carta. The Magna Carta includes the following freedoms: "Freedom of conscience and religion; Freedom of thought, belief, opinion and expression, including freedom of speech and of the press; Freedom of peaceful assembly; Freedom of association

A/B/C/D MULTIPLE CHOICE QUESTIONS

A legal procedure designed to challenge the unlawful detention of a person by the state is known as:

A. subpoena
B. detention
C. habeas corpus
D. release

357

In 1982 the Canadian Constitution was amended to include the Canadian _____.

A. Charter of Rights and Freedoms.
B. Magna Carta.
C. Liberties Manifesto.
D. Law of Citizenship.

358

The words "Whereas Canada is founded upon principles that recognize the supremacy of God and the rule of law-" are the first words in:

A. the Constitution of Canada.
B. the Magna Carta.
C. the Freedom Manifesto.
D. the Habeas Corpus Act.

359

The Canadian Charter of Rights and Freedoms was entrenched in the Constitution of Canada in the year _____.

A. 1812
B. 1814
C. 1982
D. 2009

360

A/B/C/D MULTIPLE CHOICE ANSWERS

357	**C. habeas corpus** A legal procedure designed to challenge the unlawful detention of a person by the state is known as habeas corpus.
358	**A. Charter of Rights and Freedoms.** In 1982 the Canadian Constitution was amended to include the Canadian Charter of Rights and Freedoms.
359	**A. the Constitution of Canada.** The words "Whereas Canada is founded upon principles that recognize the supremacy of God and the rule of law-" are the first words in the Constitution of Canada.
360	**C. 1982** It begins with the words, "Whereas Canada is founded upon principles that recognize the supremacy of God and the rule of law."

A/B/C/D MULTIPLE CHOICE QUESTIONS

The Canadian Charter of Rights and Freedoms summarizes fundamental freedoms, including Official Language Rights and Minority Language Educational Rights. Under this charter:

A. All languages are official languages.
B. French is the only official language.
C. English is the only official language.
D. Both French and English are official languages.

361

Men and women in Canada:

A. have different rights under the law.
B. are equal under the law.
C. are never equal under the law.
D. are only sometimes equal under the law.

362

Which of the following is not a citizenship responsibility?

A. obeying the law
B. serving on a jury
C. voting in elections
D. participating in sports

363

In Canada:

A. military service is not compulsory.
B. you must serve in the military.
C. you must serve in the Coast Guard.
D. you must serve in the fire department.

364

A/B/C/D MULTIPLE CHOICE ANSWERS

361	**D. Both French and English are official languages.** **The charter also sets out other rights relating to: Mobility rights, Aboriginal People's' Rights, and Multiculturalism.**
362	**B. are equal under the law.** **Persons who are guilty of crimes such as "honour killings" and other similar criminal acts are punished by Canadian law.**
363	**D. participating in sports** **Other citizenship responsibilities include taking responsibility for oneself and one's family, helping others in the community and protecting and enjoying our heritage and environment.**
364	**A. military service is not compulsory.** **Serving in the Canadian Forces or helping in the community is voluntary.**

A/B/C/D MULTIPLE CHOICE QUESTIONS

Canadian Aboriginal peoples migrated from Asia:

A. in the 1800's
B. in the twelfth century
C. many thousands of years ago
D. in the 1970's

365

The three groups referred to with the term Aboriginal Peoples are:

A. Comanche, Aztec and Huron.
B. Indian (First Nations), Inuit and Métis.
C. French, English, Dutch
D. Lakota, Comanche and Mayan.

366

The person who said that immigrant groups, "should retain their individuality and each make its contribution to the national character" and that immigrant groups could learn "from the other...."is:
A. John Buchan, 1st Baron Tweedsmuir and Governor General of Canada from 1935 – 1940.
B. King Henry III
C. Lord Durham
D. Sir George Cartier

367

Some Nations people live in about 600 communities:

A. on reserve land.
B. in Toronto
C. in Quebec
D. in urban centres.

368

A/B/C/D MULTIPLE CHOICE ANSWERS

365	**C. many thousands of years ago** **The Canadian Constitution contains aboriginal and treaty rights. (King George III made the Royal Proclamation of 1763 which stated the basis for negotiating treaties between the aboriginals and newcomers.)**
366	**B. Indian (First Nations), Inuit and Métis.** **(From about 1800 – 1980, children of aboriginal peoples were forced to be educated in residential schools. This led to some abuses and the schools were not successful.)**
367	**A. John Buchan, 1st Baron Tweedsmuir and Governor General of Canada from 1935 – 1940.**
368	**A. on reserve land.** **Others live off-reserve, usually in urban areas.**

A/B/C/D MULTIPLE CHOICE QUESTIONS

The name of this group means "the people." They speak the Inuktitut language and live in the arctic region.

A. Métis
B. Inuit
C. Apache
D. Acadians

369

The people that are comprised of Aboriginal and European ancestry are called:

A. Inuit
B. First nation
C. Indian
D. Métis

370

Which of the following percentages relating to Aboriginal people are correct?

A. First Nations (65%), Métis (30%), Inuit (4%)
B. First Nations (33%), Métis (33%), Inuit (33)
C. First Nations (25%), Métis (25%), Inuit (50%)
D. First Nations (40%), Métis (40%), Inuit (20%)

371

The two official languages of Canada are:

A. English and Spanish
B. English and French
C. French and Spanish
D. Spanish and English

372

A/B/C/D MULTIPLE CHOICE ANSWERS

369	**B. Inuit** The arctic is harsh. To live there, the Inuit have gathered great knowledge about the wildlife and land.
370	**D. Métis** The Métis have both English speaking and French speaking backgrounds. They also speak their own Michif dialect.
371	**A. First Nations (65%), Métis (30%), Inuit (4%)** Aboriginal peoples are those whose ancestors migrated to Canada from Asia thousands of years ago.
372	**B. English and French** (18 million English speaking "Anglophones" and 7 million French speaking "Francophones.") Most French speaking people live in the province of Quebec. One province (New Brunswick) is the only province that is officially bilingual.

A/B/C/D MULTIPLE CHOICE QUESTIONS

In 1604 French colonists started settling in the Maritime provinces. The descendants of these settlers are called _____.

A. aboriginal
B. Acadians
C. nationals
D. Anglophones

373

People of Quebec are called Quebecers. Most speak French, but about one million Anglo-Quebecers speak _____.

A. English
B. Spanish
C. Arabic
D. French

374

Recent immigrants to Canada (since 1970) come from _____.

A. Europe
B. Africa
C. Asia
D. South America

375

In two of the largest cities of Canada, English is the most widely spoken language at home, followed by the non official languages of _____.

A. Italian
B. Greek
C. Lithuanian
D. Chinese

376

A/B/C/D MULTIPLE CHOICE ANSWERS

373	**B. Acadians** Two thirds of Acadians were deported from their living area between 1755 and 1763 (during the "Great Upheaval" – during the Britain/French war).
374	**A. English** Anglo-Quebecers are descendants of Irish, Welsh, Scottish and English settlers. They are usually called English Canadians.
375	**C. Asia** Because of Canada's immigration, Canada is also spoken of as being the "land of immigrants." The most numerous people living in Canada are: English, French, Scottish, Irish, German, Italian, Chinese, Aboriginal, Ukranian, Dutch, South Asian, and Scandinavian.
376	**D. Chinese** Also, the majority of Canadians identify with the Christian faith.

A/B/C/D MULTIPLE CHOICE QUESTIONS

The first Europeans that explored Canada called the native people _____ because they believed that they were in the East Indies.

A. Europeans
B. Asians
C. Indians
D. South Americans

377

After Aboriginals came into contact with Europeans, many died of diseases to which they lacked _____.

A. contact
B. immunity
C. agreement
D. time

378

What is the name of the people that colonized Greenland (1,000 years ago) and also set foot on Newfoundland and Labrador?

A. English
B. French
C. Vikings
D. Asians

379

The name Canada comes from an Iroquoian (Indian) word "kanata," which means:

A. country
B. river
C. house
D. village

380

A/B/C/D MULTIPLE CHOICE ANSWERS

377	**C. Indians** Some Indians were hunters, farmers, nomadic and some were hunter-gatherers.
378	**B. immunity** In spite of this, in the first 200 years of Canada's history, there existed military and economic bonds between the Aboriginals and the settlers.
379	**C. Vikings** (In 1497 John Cabot (Italian immigrant to England) drew a map of Canada's east coast. Also, Jacques Cartier (French) between 1534 and 1542 claimed the land for the King of France, King Francis I).
380	**D. village** The name "Canada" first appeared on maps.

A/B/C/D MULTIPLE CHOICE QUESTIONS

In 1604 European settlements were established by French explorers Pierre de Monts and:

A. Vasco de Gama
B. Samuel de Champlain
C. Christopher Columbus
D. Vikings

381

Samuel de Champlain made an alliance with:

A. the Iroquois
B. Huron, Montagnais and Algonquin
C. the Apaches
D. the Comanche, Apaches and Blackfeet

382

The company that King Charles II (1670) granted exclusive trading rights in the Hudson Bay area was called:

A. Hudson's Bay Company
B. Fur Traders, Inc.
C. Canada Fur Trading
D. Furs of Canada Company

383

The British defeated the French in _____ in the Battle of the Plains of Abraham at Quebec City. This ended the French Empire in America.

A. 1600
B. 1759
C. 1812
D. 1845

384

A/B/C/D MULTIPLE CHOICE ANSWERS

381	**B. Samuel de Champlain** **The settlements were established on St. Croix Island and Port-Royal. (St. Croix Island is in Maine (US) and at Port-Royal in Acadia (Canada).**
382	**B. Huron, Montagnais and Algonquin** **The Iroquois and the French battled for almost a century. They made peace in the year 1701. (The Iroquois were enemies with the Huron, Montagnais and Algonquin.)** **The Aboriginal peoples and the French established a fur-trade economy. Under the leadership of leaders such as Count Frontenac, Jean Talon and Bishop Laval, the French Empire spread from the Atlantic coast (Hudson Bay) to the Gulf of Mexico.**
383	**A. Hudson's Bay Company** **Furs were often collected by traders who often travelled by canoe. They formed agreements with the First Nations. These traders are called "coureurs des bois" and "voyageurs."**
384	**B. 1759** **Brigadier James Wolfe led the British soldiers and the Marquis de Montcalm led the French soldiers. They were both killed in the battle.**

A/B/C/D MULTIPLE CHOICE QUESTIONS

The people living in the "Province of Quebec" under the English speaking British Empire are known as:

A. English
B. habitants or Canadiens
C. citizens
D. inhabitants

385

Around 1776 people loyal to the Crown fled the American colonies and settled in Nova Scotia and Quebec. These people were called _____.

A. settlers
B. escapees
C. Loyalists
D. soldiers

386

Which Act in 1791 divided the Province of Quebec into Upper Canada (present day Ontario) and Lower Canada (present day Quebec)?

A. The Constitutional Act of 1791.
B. The Freedom Act of 1791.
C. The Compromise Act of 1791.
D. The Canada Agreement Act of 1791.

387

Slavery was abolished in the province of Upper Canada in 1793. Its first Lieutenant Governor was Lieutenant Colonel John Graves Simcoe. He founded the City of York whose present day name is _____.
A. Quebec City
B. Toronto
C. Harrisburg
D. Montreal

388

A/B/C/D MULTIPLE CHOICE ANSWERS

385	**B. habitants or Canadiens** In 1774, the British Parliament passed the "Quebec Act of 1774." This act permitted the French speaking Catholic people to hold public office. This act also established French civil law and English criminal law.
386	**C. Loyalists** Some of these black Loyalists (freed slaves) settled in Nova Scotia. In 1792 some moved to Africa and established Freetown in Sierra Leone (West Africa).
387	**A. The Constitutional Act of 1791.** Upper Canada was mainly English speaking and Lower Canada was mainly French speaking. "British North America" generally referred to the two Canadas (Upper and Lower) and the Atlantic colonies.
388	**B. Toronto** In 1807 the buying and selling of slaves in Canada was abolished by the British Parliament. In 1833 it also abolished throughout the empire the buying and selling of slaves.

A/B/C/D MULTIPLE CHOICE QUESTIONS

Mary Ann (Shadd) Carey was the first woman publisher in Canada. In 1853 founded and edited the Provincial Freeman, which encouraged:

A. separation from British rule.
B. expansion of Canadian territories.
C. anti-slavery and black immigration to Canada.
D. annexation of western territories.

389

In the 1800's Canadian financial institutions began to emerge. In 1832 the _____ Stock exchange opened.

A. Johnston
B. Winnipeg
C. Toronto
D. Montreal

390

The USA invaded Canada in the year _____.

A. 1776
B. 1789
C. 1812
D. 1860

391

The rebellion of 1837-38 occurred mainly because some people thought that:

A. Canada should be divided.
B. Canada should be a dictatorship.
C. democracy was not coming fast enough to Canada.
D. Canada should join with Mexico.

392

A/B/C/D MULTIPLE CHOICE ANSWERS

389	**C. anti-slavery and black immigration to Canada.** She also encouraged the support of British rule and drinking less alcohol.
390	**D. Montreal** Before the 1800's the economy of Canada relied mostly on its natural resources (fish, timber, furs, etc.) and on farming.
391	**C. 1812** In 1813 the Americans burned government buildings in Toronto. The border between the U.S. and Canada is one of the results of the War of 1812.
392	**C. democracy was not coming fast enough to Canada.** Also, some Canadians were in favor of joining the United States.

A/B/C/D MULTIPLE CHOICE QUESTIONS

The person who proposed that Lower Canada and Upper Canada be merged and given "responsible government" was:

A. Lord Durham
B. John Cabot
C. Major General Robert Ross
D. John Graves

393

The Province of Canada was the result of the 1840 unification of:

A. Quebec and Montreal
B. Toronto and Vancouver
C. Upper and Lower Canada
D. Montreal and Toronto

394

The Dominion of Canada was established by the Fathers of Confederation in 1867. Which of following are Fathers of Confederation?

A. Lord Durham, John Cabot, Major General Robert Ross
B. Sir Étienne-Paschal Taché, Sir George-Étienne Cartier, Sir John A. McDonald
C. Sir Louis-Hippolyte La Fontaine, John Cabot, Major General Robert Ross
D. Sir Isaac Brock, John Cabot, Etienne Durham

395

On July 1, 1867 the Fathers of Confederation established Canada. July 1 was celebrated as "Dominion Day" until 1982. However today "Dominion Day" is called:

A. Unity Day
B. Canada Day
C. Constitution Day
D. Liberty Day

396

A/B/C/D MULTIPLE CHOICE ANSWERS

393	**A. Lord Durham** "Responsible government" that Lord Durham recommended meant that the ministers of the Crown in order to govern needed the support of the majority of the elected representatives of the Canadian people. (He mistakenly suggested that all Canadiens needed to be assimilated into the culture of the English Protestants.)
394	**C. Upper and Lower Canada** "Responsible government" in the Province of Canada was advanced by reformers such as Robert Baldwin, Sir Louis-Hippolyte La Fontaine and Joseph Howe. In 1848-49 responsible government was introduced in Canada by Lord Elgin, governor of United Canada.
395	**B. Sir Etienne-Paschal Tache, Sir George-Étienne Cartier, Sir John A. McDonald** Two levels of government (federal and provincial) were introduced.
396	**B. Canada Day** The term "Dominion of Canada" was suggested by Sir Leonard Tilley, one of the Fathers of Confederation, in the year 1864.

A/B/C/D MULTIPLE CHOICE QUESTIONS

Which of the following groups became part of Canada first?

A. Ontario, Quebec, Nova Scotia, New Brunswick
B. Manitoba, Northwest Territories (N.W.T.)
C. British Columbia
D. Prince Edward Island

397

Canada's first Prime Minister (1867) was:

A. Sir George-Étienne Cartier
B. Sir Sam Steele
C. Sir John Alexander Macdonald
D. Gabriel Dumont

398

This Canadien was from Quebec and a key architect of Confederation.

A. Sir George-Étienne Cartier
B. Sir Sam Steele
C. Sir John Alexander Macdonald
D. Gabriel Dumont

399

Prime Minister Macdonald in 1873 established:

A. the NWMP (North West Mounted Police).
B. Fort Garry
C. Montreal
D. Hudson's Bay Company

400

A/B/C/D MULTIPLE CHOICE ANSWERS

397	**A. Ontario, Quebec, Nova Scotia, New Brunswick (1867)** **(1867) Ontario, Quebec, Nova Scotia, New Brunswick** **(1870) Manitoba, Northwest Territories (N.W.T.)** **(1871) British Columbia** **(1873) Prince Edward Island**
398	**C. Sir John Alexander Macdonald** **Sir John Alexander Macdonald's portrait is on the $10 bill.** **On January 11 we celebrate Sir John A. Macdonald Day.**
399	**A. Sir George-Étienne Cartier** **Sir George-Étienne Cartier also was instrumental in the negotiations for the following territories to enter into Canada: Manitoba, Northwest Territories, and British Columbia.**
400	**A. the NWMP (North West Mounted Police).** **The NWMP (now RCMP: Royal Canadian Mounted Police) are Canada's national police force.** **The NWMP were established after the first Métis uprising.** **Two great Métis leaders were Louis Riel (father of Manitoba) and Gabriel Dumont.**

A/B/C/D MULTIPLE CHOICE QUESTIONS

The first French-Canadian prime minister since confederation, Sir Wilfrid Laurier, is on which the following bills?

A. $1 bill
B. $5 bill
C. $10 bill
D. $20 bill

401

The person known as "Canada's greatest soldier" is:

A. Sir Arthur Currie
B. Emily Stowe
C. John Macdonald
D. Pierre Amiens

402

The founder of the woman's suffrage movement in Canada was:

A. Emile Bronte
B. Dr. Emily Stowe
C. Nancy Baker
D. Harriet Beecher

403

On remembrance day we wear a red poppy. Remembrance Day is observed on:

A. January 21
B. April 15
C. November 11
D. June 8

404

A/B/C/D MULTIPLE CHOICE ANSWERS

401	**B. $5 bill** Sir Wilfrid Laurier encouraged people to immigrate to the West. Immigration was also helped by the railway from Sea to Sea, completed in 1885. It was built mostly by European and Chinese labour.
402	**A. Sir Arthur Currie** Sir Arthur Currie fought in WWI. Canadian troops also volunteered to fight in the South African War (1899-1902).
403	**B. Dr. Emily Stowe** Nurses were granted the right to vote in 1917 and most Canadian female citizens over 21 in 1918.
404	**C. November 11** On Remembrance Day we remember the sacrifice of 110,000 Canadians who have given their lives in wars. We wear the red poppy and observe a moment of silence. The poem "In Flanders Fields" was composed by Lt. Col. John McCrae. It was composed in 1915 and is recited on Remembrance Day.

A/B/C/D MULTIPLE CHOICE QUESTIONS

The British Commonwealth of Nations is a free association of states. It evolved:

A. in the 1700's.
B. in 1886
C. after the First Word War.
D. in 2004.

405

In this battle of WWII, one in ten of the Allied soldiers was Canadian.

A. Battle of Hastings
B. Battle of 1887
C. D-Day
D. 1976

406

The Act which guarantees health insurance coverage to Canadians is:

A. The Suffrage Act
B. The Employment Act
C. The Canada Health Act
D. The Act of Independence

407

Which Act guarantees French language rights and services in all of Canada?

A. The Suffrage Act
B. The Canada Act.
C. The Official Languages Act
D. The Commonwealth Act

408

A/B/C/D MULTIPLE CHOICE ANSWERS

405	**C. after the First Word War.** **The Commonwealth includes Australia, India, some African countries and some Caribbean countries.**
406	**C. D-Day** **In the second World War (1939-1945), more than one million Canadians and Newfoundlanders served in the military, including air and naval forces.**
407	**C. The Canada Health Act** **Unemployment insurance was introduced in 1940 by the federal government** **Education is provided by the provinces and territories.**
408	**C. The Official Languages Act** **The Quebec sovereignty movement was defeated in two referendums (1980 and 1995).**

A/B/C/D MULTIPLE CHOICE QUESTIONS

The "Group of Seven" (founded in 1920) developed:

A. a style of painting
B. military maneuvers
C. educational resources
D. political parties

409

The sport of basketball was invented by:

A. Donovan Bailey in 1886.
B. Chantal Peticlerc
C. James Naismith in 1891
D. Wayne Gretsky

410

The Canadian who invented the worldwide system of standard time zones was:

A. Alexander Graham Bell
B. Reginald Fassenden
C. Dr. John A. Hopps
D. Sir Sandford Fleming

411

The British North America Act of 1867 (now known as the Constitution Act, 1867):

A. extended health care to all Canadians.
B. made peace with the U.S.A.
C. defined the responsibilities of the provincial and federal governments of Canada.
D. provided for the Canadian railway.

412

A/B/C/D MULTIPLE CHOICE ANSWERS

409	A. a style of painting The "Group of Seven" (founded in 1920) developed a style of painting.
410	C. James Naismith in 1891 Sports in Canada are popular in all provinces. Canadian scientists have contributed greatly to the world.
411	D. Sir Sandford Fleming (Reginald Fassenden contributed to the invention of the radio. Alexander Graham Bell thought of the telephone while at his summer house in Canada. Dr. John A. Hopps invented the pacemaker)
412	C. defined the responsibilities of the provincial and federal governments of Canada. Each province has a Legislative Assembly which it elects.

A/B/C/D MULTIPLE CHOICE QUESTIONS

Canada's type of government is _____.

A. libertarian
B. a federalist dictatorship
C. a parliamentary democracy
D. socialist

413

The three parts of Parliament are: the Sovereign, the Senate, and:

A. House of Commons
B. Constitutional Convention
C. Cabinet
D. local assembly

414

In the federal government, who selects Cabinet members and is responsible for government policy and operations?

A. the Senators
B. the Assembly
C. the Prime Minister
D. the Governors

415

When a bill is considered read for the first time and is printed, it is at step 1, called the:

A. First Reading
B. Second Reading
C. Third Reading
D. Report Stage

416

A/B/C/D MULTIPLE CHOICE ANSWERS

413	**C. a parliamentary democracy** If the Cabinet ministers receive a "no-confidence" vote, they must resign.
414	**A. House of Commons** The provinces have legislatures that are comprised of the elected Assembly and the Governor of the province.
415	**C. the Prime Minister** The House of Commons is elected by the people every four years. Senators are appointed by the Prime Minister. Laws are passed by both chambers and royal assent (granted by the Governor General).
416	**A. First Reading** There are 7 steps in a bill becoming law: 1) First Reading, 2) Second Reading, 3) Committee Stage, 4) Report Stage, 5) Third Reading, 6) Senate, 7) Royal Assent.

A/B/C/D MULTIPLE CHOICE QUESTIONS

In this step, Members debate and vote on a bill:

A. First Reading
B. Second Reading
C. Third Reading
D. Report Stage

417

The minimum age at which Canadians can vote is.

A. 14
B. 18
C. 21
D. 22

418

In Canada the head of state is the Sovereign. The head of government is:

A. the Senators
B. the Assembly
C. the Prime Minister
D. the Governors

419

The three branches of government are the Executive, Legislative and:

A. the people
B. the cabinet
C. Judicial
D. committees

420

A/B/C/D MULTIPLE CHOICE ANSWERS

417	**D. Report Stage** There are 7 steps in a bill becoming law: 1) First Reading, 2) Second Reading, 3) Committee Stage, 4) Report Stage, 5) Third Reading, 6) Senate, 7) Royal Assent.
418	**B. 18** Canada is a Constitutional Monarchy. Canada's Head of State is the Sovereign. The Commonwealth has 52 member states.
419	**C. the Prime Minister** The Governor General represents the Sovereign. Each of the 10 provinces has a Lieutenant Governor (appointed by the Governor General on the advice of the Prime Minister).
420	**C. Judicial** The Premier (of each province) is similar to the Prime Minister.

A/B/C/D MULTIPLE CHOICE QUESTIONS

Members of the House of Parliament are also called:

A. MPs or Members of Parliament
B. Dukes
C. Earls
D. Commoners

421

The MP (Member of Parliament) is chosen by the voters in:

A. a province
B. an electoral district
C. a town
D. a city

422

Elections Canada, an agency of parliament produces a list of eligible voters called:

A. National Register of Electors
B. National List
C. Election List
D. National Emergency List

423

The leader of the party with the most seats in the House of Commons forms the government (after being invited to do so by the Governor General). If that party holds at least half the seats in the House of Commons, the government is called:
A. the minority government
B. the majority government
C. the government elect
D. compromise government

424

A/B/C/D MULTIPLE CHOICE ANSWERS

421	**A. MPs or Members of Parliament** Federal elections are held every 4 years (in October) following the most recent general election. The prime Minister can ask the Governor General to call an election sooner.
422	**B. an electoral district** Canada has 308 electoral districts (also called constituencies or "<u>ridings</u>"). MPs sit in the House of Commons. The minimum age to run in a federal election is 18.
423	**A. National Register of Electors** To vote in a federal election, a person must: 1. be a Canadian citizen, 2. be at least 18 (on voting day), and 3. be on the National Register of Electors.
424	**B. the majority government** (If it holds less than half the seats, it is called the minority government.) After a vote of "no confidence" the Prime Minister usually asks the Governor General to call for an election.

A/B/C/D MULTIPLE CHOICE QUESTIONS

The Cabinet is made up of the Prime Minister and the _____.

A. Assemblymen
B. Cabinet ministers
C. Senators
D. royal assembly

425

The House of Commons presently has members of four major political parties: the Liberal Party, the New Democratic Party, the Bloc Quebecois, and:

A. the Conservative Party.
B. Populist Party.
C. Green Party.
D. Independent Party.

426

On a voting ballot, what do you mark to indicate the name of the candidate of your choice?

A. AOK
B. Y
C. X
D. G

427

Laws passed by local or municipal governments are called:

A. by-laws
B. major laws
C. federal laws
D. in-laws

428

A/B/C/D MULTIPLE CHOICE ANSWERS

425	**B. Cabinet ministers** The Cabinet makes decisions on how the country is run. These decisions may be questioned by the Official Opposition (Opposing party with the most members) and by parties not in power (known as opposition parties).
426	**A. the Conservative Party.**
427	**C. X** Election results are made public on television and on the Elections Canada website (www.elections.ca).
428	**A. by-laws** Municipal or local governments have responsibilities in the following areas: policing, firefighting, emergency services, recycling programs, transportation, community affairs and community health and utilities.

A/B/C/D MULTIPLE CHOICE QUESTIONS

Presumption of innocence (everyone is innocent until proven guilty) is the foundation of:

A. our judicial system
B. our political system
C. our philosophical system
D. our executive branch

429

The highest court in Canada is:

A. Provincial Court
B. Supreme Court of Canada
C. Trial Court
D. City Court

430

Which of the following police enforce federal laws and serve as the provincial police in all territories and provinces, except Quebec and Ontario?

A. the city police
B. the Royal Canadian Mounted police
C. the town and village police
D. the military police

431

Which of the following is a symbol of government, including the courts, the legislatures, the police services, and the armed forces?

A. the parliament building
B. the Crown
C. the staff
D. Canadian currency

432

A/B/C/D MULTIPLE CHOICE ANSWERS

429	**A. our judicial system** **Courts settle disputes. Police enforce laws.** **Due process means that all the legal rights of a person must be respected by the government.**
430	**B. Supreme Court of Canada** **(Provinces have a number of lesser courts.)**
431	**B. the Royal Canadian Mounted police**
432	**B. the Crown**

A/B/C/D MULTIPLE CHOICE QUESTIONS

National Flag day is:

A. February 15
B. March 15
C. April 15
D. May 15

433

The most popular spectator sport in Canada is the:

A. baseball
B. ice hockey
C. football
D. swimming

434

The animal that is on the five cent coin is:

A. pigeon
B. eagle
C. bear
D. beaver

435

The National anthem of Canada is:

A. Our Country
B. O Canada
C. Forever Canada
D. Everywhere Canada

436

A/B/C/D MULTIPLE CHOICE ANSWERS

433	**A. February 15** National Flag day is February 15 (the Canadian flag was first raised on February 15, 1965). It has a red-white-red pattern. The Maple leaf is also a Canadian symbol. The coat of arms and the motto "A Mari Usque Ad Mare" which means "from Sea to Sea" are used on currency, public buildings and government documents.
434	**B. ice hockey** The second most popular sport is Canadian football. The sport with the most registered players is soccer.
435	**D. beaver**
436	**B. O Canada** (The "<u>Royal</u> Anthem" is sung whenever the Queen is to be honored.) Citizens who are worthy of recognition are awarded the "Order of Canada."

A/B/C/D MULTIPLE CHOICE QUESTIONS

The highest honour that a Canadian can receive is:

A. The Victoria Cross (V.C.)
B. The Medal of Honour
C. The Canadian Medal
D. The Victory Cross

437

Which of the following holiday dates is NOT correct?

A. New Year's day – January 1
B. Sir John A. Macdonald Day – February 11
C. Good Friday – Friday immediately preceding Easter Sunday
D. Easter Monday – Monday immediately following Easter Sunday

438

Which of the following holiday date is NOT correct?

A. Canada Day – July 1
B. Labour Day – First Monday of September
C. Thanksgiving Day – Second Monday of October
D. Remembrance Day – November 15

439

Today more than 75% of Canadians are employed in:

A. Manufacturing industries
B. Service industries
C. Fishing Industry
D. Entertainment industry

440

A/B/C/D MULTIPLE CHOICE ANSWERS

437	**A. The Victoria Cross (V.C.)**
438	**B. Sir John A. Macdonald Day – February 11** **Sir John A. Macdonald Day is celebrated on <u>JANUARY 11</u>.** **Also remember:** **Vimy Day – April 9** **Victoria Day – Monday preceding May 25 (Sovereign birthday)** **Fete Nationale (Quebec) June 24 (Feast of St. John the Baptist)**
439	**D. Remembrance Day – November 15** **Remembrance Day is celebrated <u>NOVEMBER 11</u>.** **Also remember:** **Sir Wilfrid Laurier Day – November 20** **Christmas – December 25** **Boxing Day – December 26**
440	**B. Service industries**

A/B/C/D MULTIPLE CHOICE QUESTIONS

The biggest trading partner of Canada is:

A. Mexico
B. England
C. U.S.A.
D. Japan

441

The second largest country in the world is:

A. China
B. U.S.A.
C. Canada
D. Brazil

442

Canada has ___ distinct regions.

A. 3
B. 4
C. 5
D. 7

443

The national capital of Canada is:

A. Montreal
B. Toronto
C. Ottawa
D. Milburn

444

A/B/C/D MULTIPLE CHOICE ANSWERS

441	**C. U.S.A.** The U.S.A. and Canadian border is the world's longest undefended border.
442	**C. Canada** Canada is bordered by the Atlantic Ocean, Pacific Ocean and the U.S.A.
443	**C. 5** The 5 regions are: 1. The Atlantic Provinces 2. The Prairie Provinces 3. The Northern Territories 4. Ontario and Quebec 5. The West Coast
444	**C. Ottawa** (In 1857 Queen Victoria chose Ottawa as the capital.)

A/B/C/D MULTIPLE CHOICE QUESTIONS

Canada has _____ provinces.

A. 8
B. 10
C. 11
D. 12

445

The population of Canada (in 2010) is approximately:

A. 20 million
B. 33 million
C. 60 million
D. 120 million

446

Which of the following is NOT the correct capital for the province or territory listed?

A. Newfoundland and Labrador – St. John's
B. Nova Scotia – Halifax
C. New Brunswick – Fredericton
D. Prince Edward Island - Albany

447

Which of the following is NOT the correct capital for the province or territory listed?

A. Quebec – Quebec City
B. Ontario – Toronto
C. Manitoba – Winnipeg
D. Saskatchewan – King

448

A/B/C/D MULTIPLE CHOICE ANSWERS

445	**B. 10** **Canada has 10 provinces and 3 territories.** **(Memorize the capitals of your province or territory and the capital of Canada.)**
446	**B. 33 million** **Most Canadians live in cities.**
447	**D. Prince Edward Island – Albany** **(The capital of Prince Edward Island is <u>Charlottetown</u>.)**
448	**D. Saskatchewan – King** **The capital of Saskatchewan is <u>Regina</u>.** **Also:** **Alberta – Edmonton** **British Columbia – Victoria** **Nanavut – Igaluit** **Northwest Territories – Yellowknife** **Yukon Territory - Whitehorse**

A/B/C/D MULTIPLE CHOICE QUESTIONS

The oldest colony and the province with the most easterly point in North America, and also known for its fisheries is the province of:

A. Prince Edward Island
B. Newfoundland and Labrador
C. Nova Scotia
D. New Brunswick

449

The only officially bilingual province is:

A. New Brunswick
B. Ontario
C. Quebec
D. Nova Scotia

450

The largest city in Canada is Toronto. It is located in the province of:

A. Quebec
B. Ontario
C. Manitoba
D. Newfoundland and Labrador

451

The two provinces known as the Prairie Provinces are:

A. Manitoba and Saskatchewan
B. Quebec and Ontario
C. Labrador and Newfoundland
D. New Brunswick and Nova Scotia

452

A/B/C/D MULTIPLE CHOICE ANSWERS

449	**B. Newfoundland and Labrador** The smallest province is Prince Edward Island. The Atlantic province with the most population is Nova Scotia.
450	**A. New Brunswick** Most people in Canada (more than half) live in Ontario and Quebec. In Quebec three-quarters of the people speak French as their first language.
451	**B. Ontario** Ontario has 12 million people and has the Niagara region.
452	**A. Manitoba and Saskatchewan** Saskatchewan is known as the "breadbasket of the world" and the "wheat province."

A/B/C/D MULTIPLE CHOICE QUESTIONS

The Prairie Province that is most populous is:

A. British Columbia
B. Alberta
C. Quebec
D. Ontario

453

The Port of Vancouver is found in the Province of:

A. Alberta
B. British Columbia
C. Toronto
D. Quebec

454

Nanavut and Yukon (Northwest Territories) contain a population of 100,000, but comprise ___ of Canada's land.

A. 1/5
B. 1/3
C. 2/6
D. 3/4

455

The highest mountain in Canada is:

A. Mount McKinley
B. Mount Logan
C. Mount Sinai
D. Mount Pacific

456

A/B/C/D MULTIPLE CHOICE ANSWERS

453	**B. Alberta** The Province was named after Princess Louise Caroline Alberta, the fourth daughter of Queen Victoria.
454	**B. British Columbia** Chinese and Punjabi are spoken often in some cities in British Columbia, next to English.
455	**B. 1/3** During the 1890's gold rush, thousands of minors came to the Yukon in search of treasure.
456	**B. Mount Logan** It is named after Sir William Logan, who also: 1. is considered to be one of the greatest scientists of Canada; 2. is a world famous geologist; and 3. founded the Geologic Survey of Canada (1842-1849).

MORE STUDY QUESTIONS

The following are our proposed answers to the sample questions asked in the study guide, and also other questions.

We suggest that you study all of these possible answers.

---

457. CANADIAN RIGHTS AND FREEDOMS are contained in which key documents?

Two key documents are:
1. **The Magna Carta (also known as The Great Charter of Freedoms)**
2. **The Constitution of Canada.**

---

458. What are some of the RIGHTS that Canadians have?

1. Canadians have the right to travel in Canada and go out or come back to Canada.

They can also choose where to live and work (called **MOBILITY RIGHTS**).

2. The Charter of Freedoms does not affect adversely any rights or freedoms that aboriginal people have. These rights are called **ABORIGINAL PEOPLE'S RIGHTS**.

3. The English language and the French language are equal in the government and in Parliament. Also, minorities have certain language educational rights. These rights are called **OFFICIAL LANGUAGE RIGHTS AND MINORITY LANGUAGE EDUCATIONAL RIGHTS.**

4. Canadians have the right to live in a pluralistic society, with each group of people contributing to the diversity and enrichment of society. This is the right to live in a country of **MULTICULTURALISM**.

---

459. What are some of the FREEDOMS that Canadians have?

Four (4) rights that Canadians have are the following:
1. Freedom of expression, thought, opinion, belief, freedom of press, and of speech
2. Freedom of association
3. Freedom of conscience and religion

4. Freedom of peaceful assembly

---

460. What is meant by the phrase "equality of men and women?"
The term **"EQUALITY OF MEN AND WOMEN"** refers to the fact that in Canada men and women have equal rights under the law. Cultural practices of other countries that promote inequality are NOT allowed in Canada. Abuse of men or women is punished by Canadian criminal law.

---

461. What are some responsibilities of good Canadian citizens?
Good citizens **TAKE RESPONSIBILITY** for themselves and their families.
Some responsibilities include:
1. voting
2. obeying the law
3. serving on a jury
4. taking responsibility for one's family and oneself.
5. volunteering in the community, or volunteering to serve or defend Canada.

---

462. Who are Aboriginals?
Aboriginal peoples migrated to Canada from Asia. They were in Canada long before the first explorers (that is, Vikings and then English speaking and French-speaking Christian settlers). Aboriginal peoples have three groups:
1. Inuit (means "the people") that live in the arctic
2. Indian (all aboriginal peoples that are not Métis or Inuit)
3. Métis (people of mixed European and Indian ancestry)

---

463. Who are the MÉTIS?
The **MÉTIS** are people of mixed European and Indian ancestry.

---

464. What does "Inuit" mean?
INUIT means **"THE PEOPLE"**.

---

465. What does "responsible government" mean?
RESPONSIBLE GOVERNMENT means that the ministers of the crown in order to govern need the consent of the majority of the elected Canadian representatives.

---

466. Who was HIPPOLYTE LA FONTAINE?
He was the first leader of the Canadas responsible government. He struggled for democracy and French language rights.

467. What did the Canadian Pacific Railway symbolize?
The **CANADIAN PACIFIC RAILWAY** symbolized Canadian unity.

468. What does "Confederation" mean?
CONFEDERATION means the birth of Canada on July 1, 1867.

469. Why is the discovery of insulin by Sir Frederick Banting important?
The **DISCOVERY OF INSULIN** by Sir Frederick Banting and Charles Best helped save 16 million lives.

470. Who is the Head of State in a Constitutional Monarchy?
In a **CONSTITUTIONAL MONARCHY** the Head of State is a hereditary King or Queen. However, the King or Queen reigns in accordance with law (the Constitution).

470. In Canada there are 3 branches of government. Name them.
The **THREE BRANCHES OF GOVERNMENT** are: the Executive, Legislative and Judicial.

471. Name the type of government that Canada has.

Canada is a **CONSTITUTIONAL MONARCHY**.

The HEAD OF STATE is a hereditary Sovereign (King or Queen). The King or Queen reigns in accordance with the Constitution of Canada.
The HEAD OF GOVERNMENT is the Prime Minister. The Prime Minister is the person who is responsible for running the government.

472. Name the highest honour that a Canadian can receive.
The **HIGHEST HONOUR** that Canadians can receive is THE **VICTORIA CROSS (V.C.)**.

473. What does a Canadian voter do on election day?
On **ELECTION DAY** you vote for the candidates of your choice.
You go to the polling station with your identification and voter information card. On the ballot (the voting sheet) you mark an "**X**" next to the candidates of your choice.

473. To be eligible to vote, a Canadian must meet the following 3 requirements:

In Canadian federal elections **A PERSON MAY VOTE** if the person:
1. is a Canadian citizen, AND
2. the person is at least 18 years old on voting day, AND
3. the person is on the voter's list.

474. After a Canadian votes, is he or she obliged to tell anyone how she or he voted?
In Canada **you are NOT obliged** to tell anyone how you voted.

475. After an election, who forms the government?
After an election **the political party with the greatest number of seats in the House of Commons** is invited by the Governor General to form a government.

476. Name your Member of Parliament.
                    The name of my Member of Parliament is:

_____

477. The Canadian government has 3 levels. Name them.

THE THREE LEVELS OF GOVERNMENT are:
1. **FEDERAL**
2. **PROVINCIAL AND TERRITORIAL**
3. **MUNICIPAL (local)**

478. What is the role of the courts in Canada?
THE ROLE OF THE COURTS in Canada is to guarantee that everyone receives due process under the law.

479. Are Canadians allowed to question the police about their service?
In Canada you **ARE ALLOWED TO QUESTION THE POLICE** about their service or conduct.

480. Name at least 2 Canadian symbols:

TWO CANADIAN SYMBOLS are:
1. The Canadian Crown
2. The National Flag
Also:
3. The Maple Leaf
4. The Coat of Arms and Motto
5. Parliament Buildings

481. Which provinces are referred to as the "Atlantic Provinces"?

The provinces that are sometimes referred to as the **ATLANTIC PROVINCES** are:
1. Newfoundland and Labrador
2. Prince Edward Island
3. Nova Scotia
4. New Brunswick

482. Name the capital of the province you live in.

The capital of the province that I live in is:

_____

483. Name THE 3 RESPONSIBILITIES OF CITIZENSHIP.

The 3 responsibilities of citizenship are:
1. Obeying the law.
2. Serving on a jury.
3. Taking responsibility for oneself and one's family.

484. Who chooses Members of Parliament?
MEMBERS OF PARLIAMENT ARE CHOSEN by the voters in their **"constituency"** (known as **"riding"**).

485. What happens after a "vote of no confidence?"
After a **vote of "no confidence"** the Prime Minister usually asks the Governor General to call for an election.

486. Where is the Port Of Vancouver located?

The Port of Vancouver is found in the Province of British Columbia.

487. When a person takes the Oath of Citizenship, he can "swear" or _____.

When a person takes the Oath of Citizenship, he can "swear" or "affirm."

488. Who do we swear allegiance to?

We swear allegiance to our Sovereign, Queen Elizabeth the Second.

489. What type of government does Canada Have?

Canada is also a constitutional monarchy.

490. What are the seven steps in a bill becoming law?

The 7 steps in a bill becoming law are: 1) First Reading, 2) Second Reading, 3) Committee Stage, 4) Report Stage, 5) Third Reading, 6) Senate, 7) Royal Assent.

491. Sir John A. McDonald Day is celebrated on which day?

Sir John A. McDonald Day is celebrated JANUARY 11.

492. What was the founder of the woman's suffrage movement in Canada?
The founder of the woman's suffrage movement in Canada was Dr. Emily Stowe.

493. Name the 2 Central Canada provinces.
The 2 Central Canada provinces are Quebec and Ontario.

494. Which 3 provinces are called the "Prairie Provinces"?
The 3 provinces that are called the Prairie Provinces are Manitoba, Saskatchewan, and Alberta.

495. The single province that is on the West Coast is?
The single province that is on the West Coast is British Columbia.

496. What is the province with the greatest population?
The province with the greatest population is Ontario.

497. In the 1890's many miners came to this Territory searching for gold.
In the 1890s many miners came to the Yukon in search for gold.

498. Why do we wear the Remembrance Day Poppy?
We wear the Remembrance Day Poppy to remember the Canadians who died in wars.

499. Who votes for Members of Parliament?

The voters in a "constituency" (also known as "riding") vote for the MP.

500. List 2 responsibilities of Canadian citizenship.

Obeying the law and serving on a jury.

(A third responsibility is taking responsibility for oneself and one's family.)

SAMPLE TEST 1

1. We swear (or affirm) allegiance to:
A. the constitution
B. the flag
C. Canada
- D. Her Majesty Queen Elizabeth the Second, Queen of Canada

2 At the Oath of Citizenship Ceremony, the applicant:
A. must write the test.
B. must answer 20 questions.
C. receives a Canadian passport.
- D. takes the Oath of Citizenship.

3. A legal procedure designed to challenge the unlawful detention of a person by the state is known as:
A. subpoena
B. detention
- C. habeas corpus
D. release

4. Men and women in Canada:
A. have different rights under the law.
- B. are equal under the law.
C. are never equal under the law.
D. are sometimes equal under the law.

5. Who said that immigrant groups, "should retain their individuality and each make its contribution to the national character" and that immigrant groups could learn "from the other, and ... while they cherish their own special loyalties and traditions, they cherish not less that new loyalty and tradition which springs from their union."

- A. John Buchan, 1st Baron Tweedsmuir and Governor General of Canada from 1935 – 1940.
B. King Henry III
C. Lord Durham
D. Sir George Cartier

6. Two Canadian official languages are:
A. English and Spanish
- B. English and French
C. French and Spanish
D. Spanish and English

7. The first Europeans that explored Canada called the native people _____ because they believed that they were in the East Indies.
A. Europeans
B. Asians
- C. Indians
D. South Americans

8. Samuel de Champlain made an alliance with:
A. the Iroquois
- B. Huron, Montagnais and Algonquin
C. the Apaches
D. the Comanche, Apaches and Blackfeet

9. Which Act in 1791 divided the Province of Quebec into Upper Canada (present day Ontario) and Lower Canada (present day Quebec)?
- A. The Constitutional Act of 1791.
B. The Freedom Act of 1791.
C. The Compromise Act of 1791.
D. The Canada Agreement Act of 1791.

10. The rebellion of 1837-38 occurred mainly because people thought that:
A. Canada should be divided.
B. Canada should be a dictatorship.
C. democracy was not coming fast enough to Canada.
D. Canada should join with Mexico.

11. Which of the following groups became part of Canada first?
A. Ontario, Quebec, Nova Scotia, New Brunswick
B. Manitoba, Northwest Territories (N.W.T.)
C. British Columbia
D. Prince Edward Island

12. The person known as "Canada's greatest soldier" is:
A. Sir Arthur Currie
B. Emily Stowe
C. John Macdonald
D. Pierre Amiens

13. The Act which guarantees health insurance coverage is:
A. The Suffrage Act
B. The Employment Act
C. The Canada Health Act
D. The Act of Independence

14. The British North America Act of 1867 (now known as the Constitution Act, 1867):
A. extended health care to all Canadians.
B. made peace with the U.S.A.
C. defined the responsibilities of the provincial and federal governments of Canada.
D. provided for the Canadian railway.

15. In this legislative step, Members debate and vote on a bill:
A. First Reading   C. Third Reading
B. Second Reading D. Report Stage

16. Elections Canada, a neutral agency of parliament produces a list called:
A. National Register of Electors
B. National List
C. Election List
D. National Emergency List

17. On a voting ballot, what do you mark to indicate the name of the candidate of your choice?
A. AOK   C. X
B. Y   D. G

18. Which of the following is a symbol of government, including the courts, the legislatures, the police services, the armed forces?
A. the parliament building
B. the Crown
C. the star
D. the flag of Maine

19. Which of the following holiday dates is NOT correct?
A. New Year's day – January 1
B. Sir John A. Macdonald Day – February 11
C. Good Friday – Friday immediately preceding Easter Sunday
D. Easter Monday – Monday immediately following Easter Sunday

20. Canada has ___ distinct regions.
A. 3   C. 5
B. 4   D. 7

END: (Answers on pg. 202)

SAMPLE TEST 2

1. Who personifies Canada?
A. every citizen
B. The Prime Minister
C. Minister of Public Works
D. our Sovereign

2. If an applicant does not pass the Citizenship Test, the applicant:
A. loses his filing fee.
B. cannot take the test ever again.
C. must sign the oath form.
D. receives a notification indicating the next steps.

3. In 1982 the Canadian Constitution was amended to include the Canadian _____.
A. Charter of Rights and Freedoms.
B. Magna Carta.
C. Liberties Manifesto.
D. Law of Citizenship.

4. Which of the following is not a citizenship responsibility?
A. obeying the law
B. serving on a jury
C. voting in elections
D. participating in sports

5. Some Nations people live in about 600 communities:
A. on reserve land.   C. in Quebec
B. in Toronto   D. in urban centres.

6. In 1604 French colonists started settling in the Maritime provinces. The descendants of these settlers are called _____.
A. aboriginals   C. nationals
B. Acadians   D. Anglophones

7. After Aboriginals came into contact with Europeans, many died of diseases to which they lacked _____.
A. contact
B. immunity
C. agreement
D. time

8. The company that King Charles II (1670) granted exclusive trading rights in the Hudson Bay area was called:
A. Hudson's Bay Company
B. Fur Traders, Inc.
C. Canada Fur Trading
D. Furs of Canada Company

9. Slavery was abolished first in the province of Upper Canada in 1793. Its first Lieutenant Governor was Lieutenant Colonel John Graves Simcoe. He founded the City of York whose present day name is _____.
A. Quebec City   C. Harrisburg
B. Toronto   D. Montreal

10. The person who suggested that Lower Canada and Upper Canada be merged and given "responsible government" was:
A. Lord Durham
B. John Cabot
C. Major General Robert Ross
D. John Graves

11. Which of the following groups became part of Canada first?
A. Ontario, Quebec, Nova Scotia, New Brunswick
B. Manitoba, Northwest Territories
C. British Columbia
D. Prince Edward Island

12. The founder of the woman's suffrage movement in Canada was:
A. Emile Bronte
B. Dr. Emily Stowe
C. Nancy Baker
D. Harriet Beecher

13. Which Act guarantees French language rights and services in all of Canada?
A. The Suffrage Act
B. The Canada Act.
C. The Official Languages Act
C. The Commonwealth Act

14. Canada's type of government is:
A. an oligarchy
B. a federalist dictatorship
C. a parliamentary democracy
D. socialist

15. The minimum age at which Canadians can vote is.
A. 14
B. 18
C. 21
D. 22

16. The leader of the party with the most seats in the House of Commons forms the government (after being invited to do so by the Governor General). If that part holds at least half the seats in the House of Commons, the government is called:

A. the minority government
B. the majority government
C. the government elect
D. compromise government

17. Laws passed by local or municipal governments are called:
A. by-laws
B. major laws
C. federal laws
D. in-laws

18. National Flag of Canada Day is:
A. February 15
B. March 15
C. April 15
D. May 15

19. Which of the following holiday date is NOT correct?
A. Canada Day – July 1
B. Labour Day – First Monday of September
C. Thanksgiving Day – Second Monday of October
D. Remembrance Day – November 15

20. The national capital of Canada is:
A. Montreal
B. Toronto
C. Ottawa
D. Milburn

END: (Answers on pg. 202)

SAMPLE TEST 3

1. Immigrants and settlers have been coming to Canada for:
A. 200 years
B. 300 years
C. 400 years
D. 500 years

2. Which of the following is false? At the ceremony, an applicant for citizenship:
A. takes the Oath of Citizenship.
B. signs a form called the "oath form".
C. is given the Canadian Citizenship Certificate.
D. must pay a citizenship fee.

3. The words "Whereas Canada is founded upon principles that recognize the supremacy of God and the rule of law-" are the first words in:
A. the Constitution of Canada.
B. the Magna Carta.
C. the Freedom Manifesto.
D. the Habeas Corpus Act.

4. In Canada:
A. military service is not compulsory.
B. you must serve in the military.
C. you must serve in the Coast Guard.
D. you must serve in the fire department.

5. The name of this group means "the people." They speak the Inuktitut language and live in the arctic region.
A. Métis
B. Inuit
C. Apache
D. Acadians

6. People of Quebec are called Quebecers. Most speak French, but about one million Anglo-Quebecers speak ____.
A. English
B. Spanish
C. Arabic
D. French

7. What is the name of the people that colonized Greenland (1,000 years ago) and also set foot on Newfoundland and Labrador?
A. English
B. French
C. Vikings
D. Asians

8. The British defeated the French in _____ in the Battle of the Plains of Abraham at Quebec City. This ended the French Empire in America.
A. 1600   C. 1812
B. 1759   D. 1845

9. Mary Ann (Shadd) Carey, the first woman publisher in Canada, in 1853 founded and edited the Provincial Freeman, which encouraged:
A. separation from British rule.
B. expansion of Canadian territories.
C. anti-slavery and black immigration to Canada.
D. annexation of western territories.

10. The Province of Canada was the result of the 1840 unification of:
A. Quebec and Montreal
B. Toronto and Vancouver
C. Upper and Lower Canada
D. Montreal and Toronto

11. Prime Minister Macdonald in 1873 established:
- A. the NWMP (North West Mounted Police).
- B. Fort Garry
- C. Montreal
- D. Hudson's Bay Company

12. The British Commonwealth of Nations is a free association of states. It evolved:
- A. in the 1700's.
- B. in 1886
- C. after the First Word War.
- D. in 2004.

13. The "Group of Seven" (founded in 1920) developed:
- A. a style of painting
- B. military maneuvers
- C. educational resources
- D. political parties

14. The three parts of Parliament are: the Sovereign, the Senate, and:
- A. House of Commons
- B. Constitutional Convention
- C. Cabinet
- D. local assembly

15. In Canada the head of state is the Sovereign. The head of government is:
- A. the Senators
- B. the Assembly
- C. the Prime Minister
- D. the Governors

16. The Cabinet is made up of the Prime Minister and the _____.
- A. Assemblymen
- B. Cabinet ministers
- C. Senators
- D. royal assembly

17. Presumption of innocence (everyone is innocent until proven guilty) is the foundation of:
- A. our judicial system
- B. our political system
- C. our philosophical system
- D. our executive branch

18. The most popular spectator sport in Canada is:
- A. baseball
- B. ice hockey
- C. football
- D. swimming

19. Today more than 75% of Canadians are employed in:
- A. Manufacturing industries
- B. Service industries
- C. Fishing Industry
- D. Entertainment industry

20. Canada has _____ provinces.
- A. 8
- B. 10
- C. 11
- D. 12

END: (Answers on pg. 202)

SAMPLE TEST 4

1 Which of the following choices is not correct? Canada is:
A. a federal state
B. a parliamentary democracy
C. a dictatorship
C. a constitutional monarchy

2. Which of the following is NOT a source of Canadian law?
A. the civil code of France
B. English common law and laws passed by the provincial legislatures and parliament
C. Great Britain's unwritten constitution
D. laws enacted by the North Atlantic Treaty Organization.

3. The Canadian Charter of Rights and Freedoms was entrenched in the Constitution of Canada in the year
____.
A. 1812
B. 1814
C. 1982
D. 2009

4. Canadian Aboriginal peoples migrated from Asia:
A. in the 1800's
B. In the twelfth century
C. many thousands of years ago
D. In the 1970's

5. The people that are comprised of Aboriginal and European ancestry are called:
A. Inuit
B. First nation
C. Indian
D. Métis

6. Recent immigrants to Canada (since 1970) come from _____.
A. Europe   C. Asia
B. Africa   D. South America

7. The name Canada comes from an Iroquoian (Indian) word "kanata," which means:
A. country
B. river
C. house
D. village

8. The people living in the "Province of Quebec" under the English speaking British Empire are known as:
A. English
B. habitants or Canadiens
C. citizens
D. inhabitants

9. In the 1800's Canadian financial institutions began to emerge. In 1832 the _____ Stock exchange opened.
A. Johnston   C. Toronto
B. Winnipeg   D. Montreal

10. The Dominion of Canada was established by the Fathers of Confederation in 1867. Which of the following are Fathers of Confederation?
A. Lord Durham, John Cabot, Major General Robert Ross
B. Sir Étienne-Paschal Taché, Sir George-Étienne Cartier, Sir John A. McDonald
C. Sir Louis-Hippolyte La Fontaine, John Cabot, Major General Robert Ross
D. Sir Isaac Brock, John Cabot, Etienne Durham

11. The first French-Canadian prime minister since confederation, Sir Wilfrid Laurier, is on which the following bills?
A. $1 bill
B. $5 bill
C. $10 bill
D. $20 bill

12. On remembrance day we wear a red poppy. Remembrance Day is observed on:
A. January 21
B. April 15
C. November 11
D. June 8

13. The sport of basketball was invented by:
A. Donovan Bailey in 1886.
B. Chantal Peticlerc
C. James Naismith in 1891
D. Wayne Gretsky

14. In the federal government, who selects Cabinet members and is responsible for government policy and operations?
A. the Senators
B. the Assembly
C. the Prime Minister
D. the Governors

15. The three branches of government are the Executive, Legislative and:
A. the people
B. the cabinet
C. Judicial
D. committees

16. The House of Commons presently has members of four major political parties: the Liberal Party, the New Democratic Party, the Bloc Quebecois, and:
A. the Conservative Party.
B. Populist Party.
C. Green Party.
D. Independent Party.

17. The highest court in Canada is:
A. Provincial Court
B. Supreme Court of Canada
C. Trial Court
D. City Court

18. The animal that is on the five cent coin is the:
A. pigeon
B. eagle
C. bear
D. beaver

19. The biggest trading partner of Canada is:
A. Mexico
B. England
C. U.S.A.
D. Japan

20. The population of Canada in 2010 is approximately:
A. 20 million
B. 33 million
C. 60 million
D. 120 million

END: (Answers on pg. 202)

SAMPLE TEST 5

1. The only officially bilingual province is:
A. New Brunswick
B. Ontario
C. Quebec
D. Nova Scotia

2. The largest city in Canada is Toronto. It is located in the province of:
A. Quebec
B. Ontario
C. Manitoba
D. Newfoundland and Labrador

3. To become a Canadian citizen, a person between the ages of _____ must have adequate knowledge of French or English.
A. 21 and 62   C. 16 and 55
B. 18 and 54   D. 21 and 54

4. The Magna Carta, signed in 1215, is also known as :
A. the Constitution
B. the amendment
C. the Great Charter of Freedoms
D. the First Law

5. The Canadian Charter of Rights and Freedoms summarizes fundamental freedoms, including Official Language Rights and Minority Language Educational Rights. Under this charter:
A. all languages are official languages
B. French is the only official language
C. English is the only official language
D. Both French and English are official languages.

6. The three groups referred to in with the term Aboriginal Peoples are:
A. Comanche, Aztec and Huron.
B. Indian (First Nations), Inuit and Métis.
C. French, English, Dutch
D. Lakota, Comanche and Mayan.

7. Which of the following percentages relating to Aboriginal people are correct?
A. First Nations (65%), Métis (30%), Inuit (4%)
B. First Nations (33%), Métis (33%), Inuit (33)
C. First Nations (25%), Métis (25%), Inuit (50%)
D. First Nations (40%), Métis (40%), Inuit (20%)

8. In two of the largest Canadian cities, English is the most widely spoken language at home, followed by _____.
A. Italian   C. Lithuanian
B. Greek   D. Chinese

9. In 1604 European settlements were established by French explorers Pierre de Monts and:
A. Vasco de Gama
B. Samuel de Champlain
C. Christopher Columbus
D. Vikings

10. Around 1776 people loyal to the Crown fled the thirteen American colonies and settled in Nova Scotia and Quebec. They were called _____.
A. settlers   C. Loyalists
B. escapees   D. soldiers

11. The USA invaded Canada in the year _____.
A. 1776
B. 1789
C. 1812
D. 1860

12. On July 1, 1867 the Fathers of Confederation established Canada. July 1 was celebrated as "Dominion Day" until 1982. However today "Dominion Day" is called:
A. Unity Day
B. Canada Day
C. Constitution Day
D. Liberty Day

13. In this battle, one in ten of the Allied soldiers was Canadian.
A. Battle of Hastings
B. Battle of 1887
C. D-Day
D. 1976

14. The Canadian who invented the worldwide system of standard time zones was:
A. Alexander Graham Bell
B. Reginald Fassenden
C. Dr. John A. Hopps
D. Sir Sandford Fleming

15. When a bill is considered read for the first time and is printed, it is at step 1, which is called the:
A. First Reading
B. Second Reading
C. Third Reading
D. Report Stage

16. Members of the House of Parliament are also called:
A. MPs or Members of Parliament
B. Dukes
C. Earls
D. Commoners

17. Which of the following police enforce federal laws and serve as the provincial police in all of Canada, except Quebec and Ontario?
A. the city police
B. the Royal Canadian Mounted police
C. the town and village police
D. the military police

18. The National anthem of Canada is:
A. Our Country
B. O Canada
C. Forever Canada
D. Everywhere Canada

19. The second largest country in the world is:
A. China
B. U.S.A.
C. Canada
D. Brazil

20. Which of the following is NOT the correct capital for the province or territory listed?
A. Newfoundland and Labrador – St. John's
B. Nova Scotia – Halifax
C. New Brunswick – Fredericton
D. Prince Edward Island - Albany

END: (Answers on pg. 202)

SAMPLE TEST 6

1. Which of the following choices is NOT correct? To become a Canadian citizen, a person must learn about:
A. U.S. history
B. geography of Canada
C. Canada's history
D. responsibilities of Canadian citizenship

2. How old does an applicant have to be to not be required to write the citizenship test?
A. 18   C. 55
B. 21   D. 34

3. Which of the following rights are included in the Magna Carta?
1. Freedom of Association
2. Freedom of conscience and religion.
A. none of them
B. both freedoms are included in the Magna Carta.
C. Only A. Freedom of Association
D. Only B. Freedom of conscience and religion

4. Canada's first Prime Minister (1867) was:
A. Sir George-Étienne Cartier
B. Sir Sam Steele
C. Sir John Alexander Macdonald
D. Gabriel Dumont

5. A patriotic Canadien from Quebec and a key architect of Confederation was:
A. Sir George-Étienne Cartier
B. Sir Sam Steele
C. Sir John Alexander Macdonald
D. Gabriel Dumont

6. The MP (Member of Parliament) is chosen by the voters in:
A. a province
B. an electoral district
C. A town
D. a city

7. The highest honour that a Canadian can receive is:
A. The Victoria Cross (V.C.)
B. The Medal of Honour
C. The Canadian Medal
D. The Victory Cross

8. Which of the following is NOT the correct capital for the province or territory listed?
A. Quebec – Quebec City
B. Ontario – Toronto
C. Manitoba – Winnipeg
D. Saskatchewan – King

9. The two provinces known as the Prairie Provinces are:
A. Manitoba and Saskatchewan
B. Quebec and Ontario
C. Labrador and Newfoundland
D. New Brunswick and Nova Scotia

10. The highest mountain in Canada is:
A. Mount McKinley
B. Mount Logan
C. Mount Sinai
D. Mount Pacific

11. The Magna Carta ensures:
A. freedom from jail and paying taxes.
B. unfair factory labor.
C. freedom from taxes only.
D. freedom of conscience and religion.

12. The oldest colony and the province with the most easterly point is North America, and also known for its fisheries is the province of:
A. Prince Edward Island
B. Newfoundland and Labrador
C. Nova Scotia
D. New Brunswick

13. The Port of Vancouver is found in the Province of:
A. Alberta
B. British Columbia
C. Toronto
D. Quebec

14. The Prairie Province that is most populous is:
A. British Columbia
B. Alberta
C. Quebec
D. Ontario

15. Who personifies Canada?
A. every citizen
B. The Prime Minister
C. Minister of Public Works
D. our Sovereign

16. Which of the following choices is not correct? Canada is:
A. a federal state
B. a parliamentary democracy
C. a dictatorship
C. a constitutional monarchy

17. The people that are comprised of Aboriginal and European ancestry are called:
A. Inuit
B. First nation
C. Indian
D. Métis

18. The two official languages of Canada are:
A. English and Spanish
B. English and French
C. French and Spanish
D. Spanish and English

19. What is the name of the people that colonized Greenland (1,000 years ago) and also set foot on Newfoundland and Labrador?
A. English
B. French
C. Vikings
D. Asians

20. The company that King Charles II (1670) granted exclusive trading rights in the Hudson Bay area was called:
A. Hudson's Bay Company
B. Fur Traders, Inc.
C. Canada Fur Trading
D. Furs of Canada Company

END: (Answers on pg. 202)

SAMPLE TEST 7

1. We swear (or affirm) allegiance to:
A. the constitution
B. the flag
C. Canada
D. Her Majesty Queen Elizabeth the Second, Queen of Canada

2 At the Oath of Citizenship Ceremony, the applicant:
A. must write the test.
B. must answer 20 questions.
C. receives a Canadian passport.
D. takes the Oath of Citizenship.

3. A legal procedure designed to challenge the unlawful detention of a person by the state is known as:
A. subpoena
B. detention
C. habeas corpus
D. release

4. Which of the following is not a citizenship responsibility?
A. obeying the law
B. serving on a jury
C. voting in elections
D. participating in sports

5. Some Nations people live in about 600 communities:
A. on reserve land.
B. in Toronto
C. in Quebec
D. in urban centres.

6. In 1604 French colonists started settling in the Maritime provinces. The descendants of these settlers are called _____.
A. aboriginals
B. Acadians
C. nationals
D. Anglophones

7. What is the name of the people that colonized Greenland (1,000 years ago) and also set foot on Newfoundland and Labrador?
A. English   C. Vikings
B. French   D. Asians

8. The British defeated the French in _____ in the Battle of the Plains of Abraham at Quebec City. This ended the French Empire in America.
A. 1600   C. 1812
B. 1759   D. 1845

9. Mary Ann (Shadd) Carey, the first woman publisher in Canada, in 1853 founded and edited the Provincial Freeman, which encouraged:
A. separation from British rule.
B. expansion of Canadian territories.
C. anti-slavery and black immigration to Canada.
D. annexation of western territories.

10. The Dominion of Canada was established by the Fathers of Confederation in 1867. Which of the following are Fathers of Confederation?
A. Lord Durham, John Cabot, Major General Robert Ross
B. Sir Étienne-Paschal Taché, Sir George-Étienne Cartier, Sir John A. McDonald

C. Sir Louis-Hippolyte La Fontaine, John Cabot, Major General Robert Ross
D. Sir Isaac Brock, John Cabot, Etienne Durham

11. The first French-Canadian prime minister since confederation, Sir Wilfrid Laurier, is on which the following bills?
A. $1 bill   C. $10 bill
B. $5 bill   D. $20 bill

12. On remembrance day we wear a red poppy. Remembrance Day is observed on:
A. January 21   C. November 11
B. April 15   D. June 8

13. In this battle, one in ten of the Allied soldiers was Canadian.
A. Battle of Hastings
B. Battle of 1887
C. D-Day
D. 1976

14. The Canadian who invented the worldwide system of standard time zones was:
A. Alexander Graham Bell
B. Reginald Fassenden
C. Dr. John A. Hopps
D. Sir Sandford Fleming

15. When a bill is considered read for the first time and is printed, it is at step 1, called the:
A. First Reading
B. Second Reading
C. Third Reading
D. Report Stage

16. Which of the following choices is not correct? Canada is:
A. a federal state
B. a parliamentary democracy
C. a dictatorship
C. a constitutional monarchy

17. The people that are comprised of Aboriginal and European ancestry are called:
A. Inuit
B. First nation
C. Indian
D. Métis

18. The two official languages of Canada are:
A. English and Spanish
B. English and French
C. French and Spanish
D. Spanish and English

19. Which of the following holiday dates is NOT correct?
A. New Year's day – January 1
B. Sir John A. Macdonald Day – February 11
C. Good Friday – Friday immediately preceding Easter Sunday
D. Easter Monday – Monday immediately following Easter Sunday

20. Canada has ___ distinct regions.
A. 3   C. 5
B. 4   D. 7

END: (Answers on pg. 202)

SAMPLE TESTS ANSWERS

Test 1

1.	D	5.	A	9.	A	13.	C	17.	C
2.	D	6.	B	10.	C	14.	C	18.	B
3.	C	7.	C	11.	A	15.	D	19.	B
4.	B	8.	B	12.	A	16.	A	20.	C

Test 2

1.	D	5.	A	9.	B	13.	C	17.	A
2.	D	6.	B	10.	A	14.	C	18.	A
3.	A	7.	B	11.	A	15.	B	19.	D
4.	D	8.	A	12.	B	16.	B	20.	C

Test 3

1.	C	5.	B	9.	C	13.	A	17.	A
2.	D	6.	A	10.	C	14.	A	18.	B
3.	A	7.	C	11.	A	15.	C	19.	B
4.	A	8.	B	12.	C	16.	B	20.	B

Test 4

1.	C	5.	D	9.	D	13.	C	17.	B
2.	D	6.	C	10.	B	14.	C	18.	D
3.	C	7.	D	11.	B	15.	C	19.	C
4.	C	8.	B	12.	C	16.	A	20.	B

Test 5

1.	A	5.	D	9.	B	13.	C	17.	B
2.	B	6.	B	10.	C	14.	D	18.	B
3.	B	7.	A	11.	C	15.	A	19.	C
4.	C	8.	D	12.	B	16.	A	20.	D

Test 6

1.	A	5.	A	9.	A	13.	B	17.	D
2.	C	6.	B	10.	B	14.	B	18.	B
3.	B	7.	A	11.	D	15.	D	19.	C
4.	C	8.	D	12.	B	16.	C	20.	A

Test 7

1.	D	5.	A	9.	C	13.	C	17.	D
2.	D	6.	B	10.	B	14.	D	18.	B
3.	C	7.	C	11.	B	15.	A	19.	B
4.	D	8.	B	12.	C	16.	C	20.	C

PROVINCES OF CANADA*

* Book interior graphics are from Wikipedia.com

CAPITALS OF PROVINCES

Provinces	Capital
Ontario	Toronto
Quebec	Quebec City
Nova Scotia	Halifax
New Brunswick	Fredericton
Manitoba	Winnipeg
British Columbia	Victoria
Prince Edward Island	Charlottetown
Saskatchewan	Regina
Alberta	Edmonton
Newfoundland and Labrador	St. John's

TERRITORIES OF CANADA

Provinces	Capital
Northwest Territories	Yellowknife
Yukon	Whitehorse
Nanavut	Iquluit

FLAG OF CANADA

GOVERNMENT

The 4 main levels of government in Canada are: 1. Municipal government, 2. Territorial government, 3. Provincial government, and 4. Federal government

1. MUNICIPAL GOVERNMENT

Name of municipality of residence	
Mayor or Reeve of municipality of residence	

2. TERRITORIAL GOVERNMENT

Commissioner (Federal government representative)	
Premier	
Territorial Representative	

3. PROVINCIAL GOVERNMENT

Lieutenant Governor (Representative of the Queen	
Premier (Head of Government):	
Provincial Party In Power	
Provincial Opposition Leader	
Provincial Representative	

4. FEDERAL GOVERNMENT

Head of State	
Governor General (the representative of the Queen of Canada	
Prime Minister of Canada	
Political Party In Power	
Leader of the Opposition	
Name of Loyal Opposition Party	
Other Opposition Parties and Leaders Are	
My MP (Member of Parliament) is	
My federal electoral district is	

IMPORTANT FACTS REGARDING VOTING

1. Eligible voters are listed in the "NATIONAL REGISTER OF ELECTORS."

2. Voters can vote earlier than election day by voting at either:
1. ADVANCE POLLS, or
2. by SPECIAL BALLOT.

3. On election day, voters vote at the POLLING STATION.

4. To indicate your choice of candidate, you mark an "X" in the circle next to the name of the candidate on the BALLOT (form).

5. You vote in SECRET.

6. You deposit the ballot in the BALLOT BOX.

7. Election results will be found (among other places) on:

www.elections.ca

DATES TO REMEMBER

DAY	DATE
New Year's Day	January 1
Sir John A. Macdonald Day	January 11
Good Friday	Friday immediately preceding Easter Sunday
Easter Monday	Monday immediately following Easter Sunday
Vimy Day	April 9
Victoria Day	Monday preceding May 25 (Sovereign's birthday)
Fête Nationale (Quebec)	June 24 (Feast of St. John the Baptist)
Canada Day	July 1
Labour Day	First Monday in September
Thanksgiving Day	Second Monday in October
Remembrance Day	November 11
Sir Wilfrid Laurier Day	November 20
Christmas	December 25
Boxing Day	December 26

CPSIA information can be obtained
at www.ICGtesting.com
Printed in the USA
BVOW09s0231191217
503190BV00004B/620/P